THE ARAB UPRISINGS

WHAT EVERYONE NEEDS TO KNOW®

THE ARAB UPRISINGS

WHAT EVERYONE NEEDS TO KNOW®

Second Edition

JAMES L. GELVIN

OXFORD
UNIVERSITY PRESS

Oxford University Press is a department of the University of
Oxford. It furthers the University's objective of excellence in research,
scholarship, and education by publishing worldwide.

Oxford   New York
Auckland   Cape Town   Dar es Salaam   Hong Kong   Karachi
Kuala Lumpur   Madrid   Melbourne   Mexico City   Nairobi
New Delhi   Shanghai   Taipei   Toronto

With offices in
Argentina   Austria   Brazil   Chile   Czech Republic   France   Greece
Guatemala   Hungary   Italy   Japan   Poland   Portugal   Singapore
South Korea   Switzerland   Thailand   Turkey   Ukraine   Vietnam

Oxford is a registered trademark of Oxford University Press
in the UK and certain other countries.

"What Everyone Needs to Know" is a registered trademark of Oxford
University Press.

Published in the United States of America by
Oxford University Press
198 Madison Avenue, New York, NY 10016

© Oxford University Press 2012, 2015

Library of Congress Cataloging-in-Publication Data
Gelvin, James L., 1951–
The Arab Uprisings : what everyone needs to know / James L. Gelvin —
Second edition.
pages cm
ISBN 978–0–19–022275–8 (paperback) — ISBN 978–0–19–022274–1 (hardback)
1. Protest movements—Arab countries—History—21st century.   2. Protest
movements—Middle East—History—21st century.   3. Arab countries—Politics and
government—21st century.   4. Middle East—Politics and government—21st century.
5. Protest movements—Middle East. I. Title.
JQ1850.A91G37 2015
909'.097492708312—dc23
2014042166

3 5 7 9 8 6 4 2
Printed in Canada
on acid-free paper

CONTENTS

ACKNOWLEDGMENTS   **xi**

1 A Revolutionary Wave?   **1**

What is the Arab world?   *1*

Is the Arab world homogeneous?   *1*

Why do Arabs identify with one another?   *2*

What was political life in the Arab world like on the eve of the uprisings?   *4*

Why have authoritarian governments been so common in the Arab world?   *7*

What was the state of the economy in the Arab world on the eve of the uprisings?   *10*

What benefits did Arab regimes originally promise their populations?   *12*

Why and how did Arab regimes renege on the promises they had made to their populations?   *16*

How did the demography of the Arab states make them vulnerable to uprisings?   *19*

How did a food crisis make Arab states vulnerable to uprisings?   *21*

Why did populations wanting change in the Arab world have to take to the streets?   *24*

Can we pinpoint the factors that caused the uprisings?   *25*

What was the spark that ignited the Arab uprisings?   *27*

Where did the demand for human and democratic rights come from?   28

How did the demand for human rights and democracy strike roots in the Arab world?   32

How pervasive was the demand for human and democratic rights in the Arab world before the uprisings of 2010–11?   34

How appropriate is the word "wave" to describe the spread of protests throughout the Arab world in 2010–11?   35

Where did the phrase "Arab Spring" come from, and how appropriate is it to describe events in the Arab world?   37

2 The Beginning: Tunisia and Egypt   39

What characteristics do Tunisia and Egypt hold in common?   39

How entrenched were the autocracies ruling Tunisia and Egypt?   42

How did the regimes in Tunisia and Egypt attempt to control their populations?   44

How widespread was corruption in Tunisia and Egypt?   44

How did the Tunisian uprising catch fire?   46

Why didn't the Tunisian uprising take place earlier?   48

Was the uprising in Egypt like that of Tunisia?   50

How did the initial phase of the Egyptian uprising play itself out?   51

What was the role of social media in the Tunisian and Egyptian uprisings?   54

Why did the Tahrir Square protesters and others adopt the tactic of nonviolent resistance?   57

What was the role of labor in the two uprisings?   59

What was the role of Islamist groups in the two uprisings?   62

What was the Egyptian Muslim Brotherhood?   64

What are salafis?   65

Why did the armies in Tunisia and Egypt refuse to put down the initial uprisings?   67

Why did the paths taken by the Tunisian and Egyptian uprisings diverge?   70

How did decisions made by governing parties in Egypt and Tunisia affect the course of uprisings there?   73

Why did the Egyptian military overthrow the Muslim Brotherhood government?   75

Do events in Egypt demonstrate that Islamist parties are incapable of rule?   79

What was political life in Egypt like after the military takeover?   81

How does the Egyptian uprising help us understand the other uprisings?   82

What are the five biggest myths about the Egyptian uprising?   84

3 Uprisings in Weak States: Yemen and Libya   86

What did the political systems of Yemen and Libya have in common before the uprisings?   86

What was political life in Yemen like before the uprising there?   86

What was political life in Libya like before the uprising there?   89

Why do political scientists consider Yemen and Libya "weak states"?   92

Why is the fact that Yemen and Libya are weak states important for understanding the uprisings there?   96

What role have tribes played in Yemen and Libya?   96

How did the uprising in Yemen evolve?   97

How did the uprising in Libya begin?   100

Was Qaddafi crazy, or crazy like a fox?   101

Why did the uprisings in Yemen and Libya turn violent?   102

Why did outside powers intervene in Libya?   103

What is "R2P"?   105

Why did efforts to fill the post-uprisings political void in Yemen and Libya flounder?   106

What are the fissures that might divide Yemen in the future?   109

Is civil war in Libya in the cards?   111

Why is al-Qaeda in Yemen?   112

Is al-Qaeda in Libya?   113

How did Libya affect American and Russian policy in Syria?   114

4 "Coup-Proofed": Bahrain and Syria   116

What do Bahrain and Syria have in common?   116

What is "coup-proofing"?   119

Why did Bahrain's February protests end so tragically?   122

What occurred in Bahrain in the wake of the crackdown?   124

How did the uprising in Syria begin?   126

Who is Bashar al-Assad?   128

How did the Syrian regime deal with the uprising?   128

How did the regime sectarianize the uprising?   130

How did the regime militarize the uprising?   131

Who is the "moderate opposition" in Syria?   132

What is the Islamist opposition in Syria like?   135

What is the "Islamic State"?   136

Have Syria's Kurds participated in the uprising?   140

What assistance has the Friends of Syria provided?   141

How have foreign powers intervened on the side of the Syrian government?   143

How has the uprising affected Syrians and Syrian society?   146

How has the Syrian uprising affected Syria's neighbors?   148

Why is a negotiated settlement for Syria improbable?   151

5 The Regional and Global Meanings of the Arab Uprisings   155

Did the Arab monarchies dodge the bullet during the uprisings?   155

What were the protests in the monarchies like?   157

What role have the Gulf monarchies played in uprisings elsewhere?   160

Why have the Gulf monarchies played such a prominent role in the uprisings? 161

Is American power in the Middle East on the wane? 164

How has the United States reacted to the Arab uprisings? 166

Did George W. Bush's "Freedom Agenda" pave the way for the Arab uprisings? 170

Have the uprisings strengthened or weakened al-Qaeda? 172

Will the state system in the Arab world survive the Arab uprisings? 175

How did the spread of the uprisings to Palestine affect the Israeli-Palestinian conflict? 178

What can history tell us about "revolutionary waves"? 180

Have the uprisings spread beyond the Arab world? 182

When will we be able to judge the significance of the Arab uprisings? 184

What conclusions might we draw from the uprisings so far? 185

NOTES 187
FURTHER READING 191
WEBSITES 193
INDEX 195

ACKNOWLEDGMENTS

The first edition of this book, which might also be subtitled "How I Spent My Summer Vacation," came about as a result of two phenomena. First, the Libyan uprising. Having completed a project on Syrian history, I decided to turn my sights 1,336 miles to the west to look at Libya—specifically how the Italian invasion of Libya in 1911 affected the inhabitants of the Arab east. Since the process of obtaining a Libyan visa was long and, to put it mildly, quirky, I had begun making travel arrangements in the fall of 2010 for a research trip the following summer. Then came the uprising, the government's brutal attempt to suppress it, and a six-month civil war, which tilted in favor of the rebels only in August 2011. Discretion being the better part of valor, I decided to abandon my travel plans and find another way to practice my craft (history) during my vacation.

The second phenomenon has to do with Los Angeles being a communications hub abounding in educational institutions and civic associations. After the Egyptian uprising demonstrated that the Tunisian uprising was no fluke, I began receiving requests for interviews and media appearances from as near as the local affiliates of the major American networks and as far away as Brasilia and Beijing. I also received requests for presentations from institutions as diverse as Pomona College and the Santa Monica Rotary Club. As of this writing, I have done nearly two hundred interviews and made close to seventy presentations. The requests for interviews and presentations forced me to think critically about what was going on in the Arab world, particularly how history informs what is going on there, and to hone a narrative that would be accessible to a variety of audiences. The result was the first edition of this book. Subsequent events, my rethinking of the "big picture," and the encouragement of my editor persuaded me to write a second edition, again with the hope of making what has become a very complex cascade of events accessible to a wide audience.

A number of people have assisted me in this project. First off, I would like to thank those who helped me research it by discovering useful sources in four languages and by helping me keep daily logs of the course of the various uprisings: Omar Elkabti, Patricia Fisher, Carol Hakim, Kathryn Kizer, Hanna Petro, and Elizabeth Waraksa. Then there were those who generously shared their knowledge, kibitzed, pointed out missteps, provided inspiration, or did any combination of the four: Ziad Abu-Rish, Asli Bali, Joel Beinin, David Dean Commins, Kristen Hillaire Glasgow, Bassam Haddad, Toby Jones, David W. Lesch, Maya Mikdashi, Sarah Shields, Susan Slyomovics, and Gwyneth Talley. Finally, there is my editor at Oxford University Press, Nancy Toff, and her assistants, Sonia Tycko and Rebecca Hecht, who saw this project through from beginning to end.

As far as a dedication is concerned, the choice is as obvious for the second edition as it was for the first: to all those who are still searching for heroes, I would suggest they look to the Arab world. Since December 2010 (and in many cases before), tens of thousands of men, women, and children have faced death on a daily basis to end the nightmare of oppression that all too many outside observers had written off as their destiny. This book is dedicated to them.

THE ARAB UPRISINGS

WHAT EVERYONE NEEDS TO KNOW®

1

A REVOLUTIONARY WAVE?

What is the Arab world?

The phrase *Arab world* might be defined in two ways. First, it refers to a geographical expanse that stretches from North Africa to the western border of Iran (west to east), and from the southern border of Turkey to the Horn of Africa (north to south). The Arab world includes twenty-two states: Algeria, Bahrain, Comoros, Djibouti, Egypt, Iraq, Jordan, Kuwait, Lebanon, Libya, Mauritania, Morocco, Oman, the Palestinian Territories (recognized in 2012 as a non-member observer state of the United Nations), Qatar, Saudi Arabia, Somalia, Sudan, Syria, Tunisia, the United Arab Emirates, and Yemen. The predominant language in the region is Arabic.

The phrase *Arab world* also refers to the cultural world in which the inhabitants of the region, and others who identify with that cultural world, live.

Is the Arab world homogeneous?

Most inhabitants of the Arab world are Arabic-speaking Muslims. Nevertheless, the term *Arab world* masks the fact that the inhabitants in the region are not homogeneous. For example, Muslims are divided into two main branches, Shi'is and Sunnis. The split between the two branches of Islam occurred early on in Islamic history over a dispute about who should lead the Islamic community after the death of the prophet Muhammad. Over time, each branch also developed its own sets of rituals, traditions, and beliefs. Most Arabs are Sunni, but two Arab countries (Iraq and Bahrain) have Shi'i majorities, and there are substantial numbers of Shi'is in Lebanon, Yemen, Kuwait, and Saudi Arabia. Since both rulers and their opponents in the Arab and wider Islamic worlds sometimes exploit the Sunni-Shi'i divide for their own benefit, it is necessary to know that there is a difference between the two branches of Islam. Knowing the contrasting sets of rituals, traditions, and beliefs is irrelevant for understanding the uprisings.

In addition to Shi'is and Sunnis, there are other Muslim sects in the Arab world. For example, the ruling group in Syria draws from the Alawite sect, which comprises about 13 percent of the Syrian population. There is also a substantial Christian population in the Arab world, including Maronite Christians in Lebanon, Coptic Christians in Egypt, and Orthodox Christians throughout the region.

Linguistic and ethnic minorities also live in the Arab world. Berbers, for example, make up about half the population of Morocco and about a third of the population of Algeria. Tunisia and Libya host Berber communities as well. Kurds living in the Arab world inhabit Syria and Iraq. Both groups have their own languages. Discrimination (and worse) has increased the sense of Berber and Kurdish identity among members of each group.

Why do Arabs identify with one another?

One of the most interesting aspects of the Arab uprisings has been how the actions of Egyptians, for example, captured the imagination of the inhabitants of Libya, Yemen, Syria, and elsewhere. Besides a shared language, a number of factors have increased the likelihood that the inhabitants of the region would identify with a broader Arab community. There is a sense of shared history and experiences that school systems and intellectuals encourage. There is poetry, (Egyptian) soap operas, and movies that Arabs throughout the region, and throughout the world, share. This is why the adage "Egyptians write books, Lebanese publish them, and Iraqis read them" rings true. There are regional associations, such as the Arab League and the Gulf Cooperation Council; regional development funds, such as the Arab Monetary Fund and the Arab Fund for Social and Economic Development; and a few lingering pan-Arab political parties, such as the ruling Baath Party of Syria, whose slogan remains "unity, freedom, socialism" (even if its actual commitment to unity is no more serious than its current commitment to socialism). There is the widespread opposition to American activities in the region, notably the 2003 invasion of Iraq and America's backing of Israel, which unites many of the inhabitants of the region, as well as the widespread support for the Palestinian cause. And there is the remarkable growth of Arabic-language media, such as the satellite television channel al-Jazeera, which began broadcasting in 1996 and remains the most popular source for news in the region. During the Egyptian uprising, more Egyptians got their news from the Qatar-based channel than from any other news source.

It is important to differentiate between, on the one hand, what might be called an "imagined Arab community" that exists in the heads of those who identify themselves as Arab and, on the other, Arab nationalism. Just because people might identify themselves as Arab does not mean they necessarily want to renounce their Egyptian or Lebanese citizenship, for example, in favor of citizenship in a pan-Arab state. As a matter of fact, the (pan-)Arab nationalism of the 1950s, which politicians promoted to thwart real and imagined "imperialist conspiracies," has for the most part dissipated over the decades as more and more people came to identify with the states in which they live. As recent events in the region attest, however, an Arab identity has not dissipated. This is one reason the inhabitants of the region have followed the uprisings in neighboring countries with such interest and, in some cases, sought to emulate them.

What was political life in the Arab world like on the eve of the uprisings?

In 2000, the Regional Bureau for Arab States of the United Nations Development Programme commissioned a group of scholars and policy makers to assess the state of human development in the Arab world. It published the first *Arab Human Development Report* in 2002, then followed it up with four others.[1] Overall, the reports provide a scathing assessment of political, economic, and social conditions in the Arab world in the period leading up to the uprisings.

In terms of politics, the 2002 report begins its assessment in this manner:

> There is a substantial lag between Arab countries and other regions in terms of participatory governance. The wave of democracy that transformed governance in most of Latin America and East Asia in the 1980s and Eastern Europe and much of Central Asia in the late 1980s and early 1990s has barely reached the Arab States. This freedom deficit undermines human development and is one of the most painful manifestations of lagging political development.

The reports cite a number of characteristics political systems in the region held in common on the eve of the uprisings:

- When it came to civil liberties, political rights, and independence of media, only Jordan ranked above the international mean (Kuwait ranked exactly at the mean).

- When it came to the quality of public services and the bureaucracy and independence of civil service, only eight of the twenty Arab states surveyed ranked above the international mean.
- When it came to public perceptions of corruption (graft, bribery, cronyism), ten out of the seventeen Arab states surveyed ranked above the international mean.
- The 2004 report categorized almost all Arab states as "black-hole states," in which the executive branch of the government is so powerful that it "converts the surrounding social environment into a setting in which nothing moves and from which nothing escapes."
- In states in which there was no dynastic succession (such as Algeria, Tunisia, Egypt, and Yemen), presidents regularly modified constitutionally mandated term limits. In Syria, the rubber-stamp parliament amended the constitution so that the underage son of the former president might assume the presidency.
- To garner support, most Arab governments resorted to the "legitimacy of blackmail" (more accurately rendered "legitimacy by blackmail"); that is, most presented themselves as the only bulwark standing between the citizenry and Islamism or chaos. (The terms *Islamism* and *Islamic movements* embrace a grab bag of associations, parties, and governments that seek to order their societies according to what they consider to be Islamic principles. The term *Islamist* refers to those who profess those principles. Some Islamists choose to participate in politics to achieve this end; others do not. Some believe Islamic principles provide them with a strict roadmap to be followed without deviation; others treat those principles more gingerly.)
- Most Arab states tightly restricted the formation of political parties. For example, interior ministers or government committees in Egypt, Yemen, Tunisia, and Jordan had to authorize the formation of any new party. The

Gulf states and Libya dealt with the issue of political parties simply by banning them.

- Seventeen of the nineteen Arab states surveyed required newspapers to be licensed; there was pre-censorship in eleven states.
- Syrians had been living under a state of emergency since 1963, Egyptians since 1981, Algerians since 1992, Iraqis since 2004, Palestinians since 2007, and Sudanese since 2008 (2005 in the Darfur region of Sudan). A state of emergency strips citizens of such fundamental rights as habeas corpus and the right to assemble, authorizes extraordinary courts and suspension of constitutions, and expands even further the powers of the bloated executive branch of government. Although some constitutions guaranteed such fundamental rights as the sanctity of the home and freedom of expression, most guarantees of this kind were empty promises. In some states, the constitution was ambiguous when it came to rights. Other constitutions delegated the definition of rights to the government. And still other constitutions subordinated rights to an official ideology (such as to the principles of Arab socialism) or national unity.
- In its 2008 report, the Arab Organization for Human Rights cited seven states—Iraq, Syria, Egypt, Saudi Arabia, Morocco, Jordan, Kuwait—and the governing authorities in the West Bank and Gaza for regularly torturing interned prisoners; the United Nations High Commission for Human Rights also threw in Algeria, Bahrain, Morocco, and Tunisia, for good measure.
- "State security courts," operating with unclear jurisdictional limits, imprecise procedural guidelines, and no oversight, existed in a number of Arab states. Not that it always mattered: eleven states (Bahrain, Egypt, Jordan, Lebanon, Libya, Mauritania, Saudi Arabia, Sudan, Syria, Tunisia, Yemen) allowed extrajudicial detentions.

As far as political participation is concerned, on the eve of the uprisings *The Economist* reported that not one Arab state fit into the categories of "full" or even "flawed" democracies according to its annual "Democracy Index."[2] The highest ranked Arab state was Lebanon, whose score placed it no. 86 among 163 states worldwide. Along with Palestine and Iraq (nos. 93 and 111, respectively), it was one of only three states in the region that fell into the category "hybrid democracies." In hybrid democracies, elections have substantial irregularities, there is widespread corruption, and civil society is weak. *The Economist* placed the remaining nineteen members of the Arab League within the category of "authoritarian regimes." Of these, the lowest ranked was Saudi Arabia, which tied with Equatorial Guinea for the dubious distinction of sixth most undemocratic state in the world. Overall, the Arab world had the lowest composite score of any region.

Why have authoritarian governments been so common in the Arab world?

For years, historians and political scientists speculated about the cultural or social origins of authoritarianism in the Arab world. Some pointed to Islam, arguing that it was not compatible with democracy or human rights. Others looked to family structure, arguing that a state dominated by a single (male) figure simply reproduced the patriarchy of the typical Arab family.

Today, few historians and social scientists take these explanations, or any single explanation, seriously. There is no reason to assume that Islam is any more or less compatible with democracy and human rights than Christianity or Judaism, for example. There is also no reason to assume that all Muslims approach their Islam in the same way, read the same meanings into their Islam, or even apply at all principles derived from Islam in their daily lives. Then there are counterexamples, such as Indonesia (the world's most populous

Muslim country) and Turkey; both are democracies, although with flaws (increasingly noticeable in the case of Turkey). And a state is not simply a family writ large.

Although there is no single explanation for the prevalence of authoritarian governments in the Arab world, historians and political scientists have offered two partial explanations with which many experts agree. The first has to do with the Arab state's control over resources, the second with American foreign policy.

States in the Arab world are highly dependent on a source of revenue called by economists "rent." Economists define rent as income acquired by states from sources other than taxation. Some economists call states that are dependent on rent for a certain proportion of their income "rentier states"; others call them "allocation states" because the states distribute the rent they receive to favored clients and projects.

The most lucrative source for rent in the Arab world is, of course, oil. Some Arab states derive well over 90 percent of their revenues from oil. But even Arab states not usually associated with oil production, such as Egypt and Syria, have an inordinate dependence on rent. In 2010, rent accounted for 40 percent of Egypt's revenue and 50 percent of Syria's. In the case of the former, the sale of oil provided $11 billion to the national treasury, but there were other sources of rent as well. These included American aid (about $1.6 billion) and Suez Canal tolls (about $5 billion). Syria has traditionally derived rent both from oil and from other states that fear its ability to cause trouble in the region (or that wish to encourage this ability).

In no other region of the world are states as dependent on rent as they are in the Arab world. And access to rent not only means that the state does not have to go hat in hand to its citizens for revenue, it also ensures that the state will be the dominant economic actor. This enables the state to attach itself to the population through ties of patronage. It also enables the state to buy off dissent. It was thus not out of character when, in the wake of the uprisings in Tunisia and Egypt and unrest at home, other states in the Arab world attempted to bribe their populations by offering them social benefits, pay raises, or higher government subsidies on basic commodities in order to buy social peace. In sum, rent reinforces a relationship between the state and the citizens of the state that can be summed up in the phrase "benefits for compliance."

The second partial explanation for the prevalence of authoritarian rule in the Arab world is American foreign policy. The United States did not have much of a policy toward the region until the immediate post–World War II period. American engagement with the region thus coincided with the onset of the cold war, which defined American goals there. Throughout the cold war, the United States sought to attain six goals in the region: prevent the expansion of Soviet influence; ensure Western access to oil; secure the peaceful resolution of conflicts and the maintenance of a regional balance of power; promote stable, pro-Western states in the region; preserve the independence and territorial integrity of the state of Israel; and protect the sea lanes, lines of communications, and the like connecting the United States and Europe with Asia.

Authoritarian regimes were useful in achieving all these goals. For example, American policy makers believed only strong, authoritarian regimes could bring about the rapid economic development necessary to prevent their populations from "going communist." Only strong, authoritarian regimes such as that in Egypt could sign peace treaties with Israel in the face of popular opposition to those treaties. And only strong, authoritarian regimes that maintained a regional balance of power could ensure the uninterrupted supply of oil to the United States and its allies.

American support for autocrats was both direct and indirect. The United States directly and indirectly supported military officers who seized power in states throughout the region from the late 1940s through the 1960s. For example, the United States backed (some say sponsored) the first post-independence coup d'état in Syria—the first coup in the Arab world following World War II—which overthrew a democratically elected government. And, of course, the United States directly and indirectly supported a host of autocratic kings and emirs. This began even before the end of World War II, when Saudi Arabia became the only neutral state to receive Lend-Lease assistance.

When the cold war ended, the United States maintained five of its six policy goals in the region; containing the Soviet Union, which was dismantled in 1991, was, of course, no longer necessary. Hence, the United States maintained its support for authoritarian regimes as well. Thus it was that the United States headed the coalition liberating Kuwait from Iraq in 1991. And after 9/11, the United States added another policy goal that turned out to be a further boon to friendly autocrats: the United States declared a global war on terrorism. Autocrats such as Hosni Mubarak of Egypt, Ali Abdullah Saleh of Yemen, and even Muammar Qaddafi of Libya managed to put themselves on the side of angels by agreeing to accept and interrogate under torture suspected terrorists (Mubarak), allow the United States to fight the war on terror on his country's soil (Saleh), and renounce weapons of mass destruction (Qaddafi). Although President George W. Bush announced his "freedom agenda" in 2003—a professed commitment to "drain the swamp where terrorism breeds"[3] by promoting democratic change in the region—the United States stuck with Mubarak and Saleh well past their expiration date.

What was the state of the economy in the Arab world on the eve of the uprisings?

The Arab world includes states such as Qatar, which in 2010 boasted an annual per capita income of $88,232 (for the approximately 20 percent of the inhabitants who were citizens, not guest workers), and Yemen (whose population earned an annual per capita income of about $1,000 the same year). Simply put, states in the Arab world run the gamut when it comes to wealth and poverty. Overall, oil exporters tend toward the wealthy side of the spectrum, while states whose primary source of income is not oil tend toward the poorer side. It is thus difficult to generalize about economic conditions. But it is also necessary to try, since the uprisings that have spread throughout the Arab world are about economic as well as political conditions. This is the reason why autocrats commonly attempted to prevent or defuse protests by making economic concessions to their populations—a sure sign that they recognize the role played by economic issues in promoting dissatisfaction.

In his address on the uprisings in May 2011, President Barack Obama made the point that economic assistance to Tunisia and Egypt would be necessary to ensure a smooth transition to democracy. He also stated that such assistance would be a topic at the upcoming meeting of eight industrialized countries (the G-8). In preparation for that meeting, the International Monetary Fund (IMF) put together a report on the state of the economies in the Middle East and North Africa.[4] The report paints a fairly bleak picture:

- Over the course of the previous three decades, the growth of the GDP in the region averaged 3 percent, while the GDP in the rest of the developing world grew at the rate of 4.5 percent. (GDP—or gross domestic product—is the total market value for finished goods and services produced within a state or territory.) Between 1980 and 2010, per capita GDP grew at a rate of 0.5 percent annually, well below that of the 3 percent growth that marked the rest of the developing world. To absorb the unemployed and new entrants to the job market, the annual GDP would have to grow at a rate of 7.5 percent.
- With the exception of oil and gas, exports have remained flat in recent decades. The remainder of the developing

world has more than doubled its share of the international market since 1980. The situation looks even worse when exports from oil importers in the region are compared with exports from other regions. In 2009, their exports reached only 28 percent of GDP, compared with 56 percent for the Asia Pacific region.

- Close to 60 percent of the region's exports go to Europe. This indicates two problems. First, the only comparative advantage the region has is its proximity to Europe. Second, the region is isolated from the global economy in general and from emerging markets such as China in particular. (Other sources assert that outside sub-Saharan Africa, the region is the least globalized in the world.)
- The number of jobs grew 2 percent annually between 2000 and 2007. Overall, unemployment in countries for which data are available—Egypt, Jordan, Lebanon, Syria, and Tunisia—hovered between 10 and 12 percent (other sources put the unemployment rate as high as 15 percent).
- Overall, the report asserted that oil importing states would need foreign grants and loans to the tune of $160 billion during 2011–2013 to meet their obligations.

What benefits did Arab regimes originally promise their populations?

Most states in the Arab world received their independence at roughly the same time, during the post–World War II period. There was variation in government forms, of course. In many cases, although not all, this had to do with the identity of the colonial power that had been present before independence. The British, the preeminent power in Egypt, Jordan, Iraq, and the Gulf, generally left behind monarchies (Egypt was a kingdom until 1953, Iraq until 1958). The French, the preeminent power in North Africa, Syria, and Lebanon, left behind a short-lived monarchy in Tunisia and another in Morocco, along with republics elsewhere.

In spite of the variation in government forms, however, the ruling bargains states struck with their populations were roughly the same. (The term *ruling bargain* is a metaphor used by political scientists to refer to the accommodation reached between states and the citizens they govern.) States played a major role in the economy. They did this to force-march economic development, expand employment opportunities, reward favored elements of the population, and gain control over strategic industries. States also provided a wide array of social benefits for their populations, including employment guarantees, health care, and education. In addition, states subsidized consumer goods.

There were a number of reasons states in the region—and, indeed, throughout the developing world—adopted these policies. The United States encouraged them to do so, believing that a combination of economic development and welfare would create stable, pro-Western states. So did international financial institutions, such as the World Bank and the IMF, and a legion of development experts who passed on cookie-cutter policies wherever they went. These policies fit the economic paradigm popular at the time, one that gave pride of place to full employment and rising standards of living as the two indicators of economic success. Governments, it was believed, could guide resources to ensure both goals were reached more effectively in environments where markets were not well developed.

A third factor leading to the adoption of these economic policies was the logic of decolonization. Before independence, imperial powers set economic policy, mainly for their own benefit. With independence, states asserted their economic rights to make up for lost time and attempted to win support through the redistribution of national wealth. Some states— Egypt, post-independence Algeria, Libya, Iraq, Syria at various times, and others—justified their policies using a populist discourse that extolled anticolonialism and the virtues of the revolutionary masses. In those states, the old regime that young military officers replaced represented collaboration with imperialists, feudalism, and corruption. Other states— Jordan and Saudi Arabia, for example—appealed to tradition or efficiency. Whether "revolutionary" or reactionary, however, Middle Eastern governments came to the same destination, although via different routes.

The case of Egypt was most dramatic, but not atypical. Using resources derived from widespread nationalizations (including the nationalization of the Suez Canal in 1956), a $42.5 million loan from the IMF, and $660 million in aid packages from the United States, Egypt adopted a program its leader, Gamal Abd al-Nasser, called "Arab socialism." Under Arab socialism, the state became the engine of the economy. By the mid-1960s, the Egyptian government owned and ran banks, insurance companies, textile mills, sugar-refining and food-processing facilities, air and sea transport, public utilities, urban mass transit, cinemas, theaters, department stores, agricultural credit institutions, fertilizer producers, and construction companies.

If measured by profit, state control over so much of the economy was highly inefficient. But the success or failure of Arab socialism cannot be measured in terms of efficiency alone. By administering so many productive and commercial establishments, the Egyptian state (and other states that went down a similar path) was able to allocate resources for its own purposes and gain control over industries it deemed vital for national development. Furthermore, the Egyptian government significantly reduced the ranks of the unemployed—even if the government had to hire many of the unemployed itself. For example, in 1961 the Egyptian government passed the Public Employment Guarantee Scheme, which, as the name suggests, guaranteed every university graduate a job in the public sector. The scheme was amended three years later to include all graduates of secondary technical schools. The result was as one might expect: the Egyptian bureaucracy, never a pretty sight, swelled from 350,000 in 1952 to 1.2 million in 1970. Although the government repealed the bill in 1990 after IMF prodding, the bureaucracy continued to grow. As of 2008, the government employed approximately 5 million Egyptians.

The Egyptian government used economic incentives to gain the compliance of the citizenry and reward those sectors of society it claimed to represent. Declaring an education to be a right for every citizen, for example, Nasser eliminated fees at Cairo University, after which enrollment skyrocketed (and standards declined, as they did when health care was nationalized). The state also attempted to keep household commodities affordable by furnishing subsidies for many of them, including basic foodstuffs, petroleum products, electricity, and water. As of 2009–10, subsidies, along with social benefits such as health care and education, still represented close to 42 percent of Egyptian government expenditures. Subsidies on household commodities alone accounted for about 23 percent.

Within this context, Arab policy makers came up with new definitions for democracy and democratic rights. Nasser, for example, differentiated between something he called "reactionary democracy" and his own "integral democracy." For Nasser, the reactionary democracy of the old regime was hopelessly flawed; although it promised political rights for all, the wealthy and powerful found ways to manipulate the system for their own ends. The result was rule by the few and economic exploitation of the many. Nasser's integral democracy, on the other hand, equated freedom with economic justice. And since the state was the expression of the "popular will" of the "progressive classes," it was up to the state to guarantee this economic justice. For Nasser, then, political pluralism was incompatible with the developmental and social justice goals of an activist Egyptian state.

In Egypt and throughout the Arab world, populations embraced the part of the ruling bargain that covered the state's responsibility for ensuring their welfare (this is not to say they necessarily embraced the second part of the bargain, which stipulated unquestioned submission to the dictates of the state). The 2004 *Arab Human Development Report* cites polls taken in Jordan, Lebanon, Palestine, Morocco, and Algeria on what sorts of freedom the populations expected their states to guarantee. Alongside and sometimes topping such political freedoms as the "right to form political opposition groups" and the "choice of central government leaders through free and fair elections," respondents listed "freedom from hunger," or "freedom from inadequate income," and the like. But these freedoms came at a price: according to World Bank data, average economic growth in Egypt, for example, was 7.52 percent between 1959 and 1964. This was the period in which the Egyptian government was first taking on the obligations of Arab socialism. During the 1964–73 period, when Arab socialism was at its height, growth declined to 2.85 percent.

Why and how did Arab regimes renege on the promises they had made to their populations?

Toward the end of the 1970s, governments in the Arab world began attempting to renegotiate the ruling bargain. They had to. After the price of oil spiked first in 1973 and then again in 1979, it plummeted. All Arab states had benefited from high oil prices, producers and nonproducers alike. Oil producers subsidized the ruling bargains of their less-fortunate brethren. They did this through grants and loans on the one hand, and by providing job opportunities to the populations of labor-rich, but oil-poor, Arab states on the other. When oil prices began their rapid descent in the 1980s, governments had to retrench.

Two factors made matters even worse. First, a number of Arab states—Algeria, Egypt, Jordan, Syria, Morocco, Yemen, and Sudan being the most prominent—had borrowed heavily in flush times when interest rates were low and then continued to borrow to pay debt service, maintain what they could of their increasingly tattered ruling bargain, or both. The debt burdens were so massive that one economist referred to the region as part of a "Mediterranean debt crescent."[5] Second, times had changed, and so too had the prevailing economic paradigm. State-guided economic development was out, as was public ownership of manufacturing and commercial ventures. Neoliberalism was in.

Neoliberalism is the name given to a market-driven approach to economics in which the role of the state is kept to a minimum. Although often identified with Ronald Reagan in the United States and Margaret Thatcher in the United Kingdom, the roots of neoliberalism go back to the early 1970s, when the United States took a combative approach to demands made by developing nations for greater control of the raw materials they produced, as well as for a greater role in deciding international economic policy. When in 1973 oil producers gained control of the pricing and ownership of oil—acts that led to higher oil prices and stagnant economies and inflation in the developed world—the United States pushed back, decrying any and all political interference with the market. The debt crisis of the 1980s, which affected much of the developing world, presented the United States with a golden opportunity to push the new paradigm: states that not so long before had asserted their economic rights were now begging international banking institutions for debt relief.

Debt relief was forthcoming—but at a price. In return for debt relief and access to fresh capital from international lenders such as the IMF and the World Bank, states had to undertake immediate steps to stabilize their economies, then longer-term measures to ensure fiscal health. IMF and World Bank experts demanded states cut expenditures, liberalize trade, balance their budgets, remove price controls, deregulate business, privatize public enterprises by selling them off to the highest bidder, and end across-the-board subsidies on consumer goods. In place of across-the-board subsidies, international lending institutions recommended that states grant subsidies "targeted" only to the very poor. In other words, governments were to shred the ruling bargains they had struck with their populations.

Neoliberal policies got their tentative start in the Arab world in December 1976, when Egypt negotiated a $450 million credit line with the IMF, which also gave Egypt the wherewithal to postpone $12 billion in foreign debt. In return, Egypt cut $123 million in commodity supports and $64 million from direct subsidies. The result was what one might imagine: two days of bloody rioting in which eighty to one hundred protesters died and twelve hundred were arrested. Similar "IMF riots" broke out in Morocco (1983), Tunisia (1984), Lebanon (1987), Algeria (1988), and Jordan (1989, 1996) after the IMF attempted to impose conditions on loans and loan guarantees.

Initially, states backpedaled. The IMF also modified its demands. States began to apply neoliberal policies in earnest only in the late 1980s, after a "lost decade" of virtually no growth. In Egypt, serious "economic reform" did not really begin until 2004 with the appointment of the "cabinet of businessmen." Libya began its first wave of privatizations in 2003 and followed them up with cuts in subsidies a year later. And it was not only the IMF that was responsible for the spread of neoliberalism in the region: Saudi Arabia and Syria, for example, voluntarily adopted measures associated with neoliberalism. Saudi Arabia did so in order to join the World Trade Organization; Syria, as part of its fruitless quest to join the Euro-Mediterranean Free Trade Area. The fact that such entry requirements existed in the first place demonstrates the global predominance of the neoliberal economic paradigm.

In most states, the overall effect of neoliberal policies was to overlay a jury-rigged market economy on top of an inefficient command economy. And some policies had effects different from their intentions. Privatization, for example, did not lead to capitalism but rather to crony capitalism, as regime loyalists took advantage of their access to the powerful to gain ownership of sold-off state assets. Thus it was that in Egypt a friend of the son of the president came to control 60 percent of the steel industry, while in Syria the first cousin of the president gained control over the mobile communications giant Syriatel, which, in turn, controlled 55 percent of the market. Both became popular symbols of regime corruption during the uprisings.

Even though states in the region enjoyed high growth rates during the past decade, they also experienced greater income inequalities. This, in part, explains the participation of large numbers of middle-class, professional youths in uprisings throughout the region. While states have stripped members of this cohort of the "middle-class welfare" benefits their parents had enjoyed and condemned many to fend for themselves in the ranks of the un- and underemployed, they are denied both benefits targeted to the very poor and entry into the ranks of the very privileged. It also explains the upsurge in labor activism in various places in the Arab world and the prominent role played by labor in the uprisings in such places as Tunisia and Egypt. Or, as the last pre-upsurge finance minister of Egypt put it, "We do not have a constituency for reform at the street level."[6]

How did the demography of the Arab states make them vulnerable to uprisings?

In 2010, approximately 60 percent of the population of the Arab world was under the age of thirty, and the broader Middle East and North African region was second only to sub-Saharan Africa in the percentage of youth within that bracket. Demographers call what took place in the region a "youth bulge." To a certain extent, the current youth bulge might be attributed to the successes of states in the region. Historically, youth bulges occur as a stage in the process of moving from a population characterized by high rates of fertility and mortality to a population characterized by low rates of fertility and mortality. This transformation most frequently accompanies a rise in the standard of living. If such a transformation takes place at an even rate, there will be no youth bulge. But most often it does not.

Mortality has been steadily declining in the Arab world for decades, if not longer, in large measure as the result of improvements in health care, education, public health, and sanitation. Fertility, on the other hand, did not begin to decline until the decades of the 1960s and 1970s. Population growth thus peaked in the 1980s as those born in the sixties and seventies entered their childbearing years. The result is the current youth bulge.

There is another statistic, however, that is more telling about the current state of the Arab world than the percentage of those under the age of thirty: the percentage of those between fifteen and twenty-nine, the period during which youths begin entering the job market and, more commonly in the case of women, marriage.[7] On the eve of the uprisings youths between fifteen and twenty-nine made up 29 percent of the population in Tunisia, 30 percent in Egypt, and 34 percent in Libya. Across the region, youth made up approximately 25 percent of the unemployed (30 percent among women).

But even this statistic has to be taken with a grain of salt. As might be expected, the youth unemployment rate has been much higher in states whose exports of oil are either minimal or nonexistent. Before the uprising, youth unemployment in Egypt was 43 percent, for example, and in Tunisia it was 30 percent. Furthermore, the statistics on employment do not include those who have given up on finding work (the "discouraged unemployed") and those who work part-time but who wish to work more hours. In Egypt, for example, almost 60 percent of youths eighteen to twenty-nine left the labor force (in the case of women it was 83 percent). And when it comes to employment, education affords little advantage. As a matter of fact, in Egypt young people with college degrees have traditionally ranked highest among the unemployed of any sector of youth, and in pre-uprising Syria a vast majority of college graduates

spent at least four years looking for employment before landing a job.

The lack of employment opportunities for young people in
the Arab world has given rise to a phenomenon one political
scientist calls "waithood," a period in which youths "wait for
(good) jobs, wait for marriage and intimacy, and wait for full
participation in their societies."[8] Men in particular delay marriage until they become solvent enough to pay the customary
expenses associated with marriage and can support a family.
As a result, life is put on hold, and the average age for marriage
among men in the Arab world is the highest of any region of
the world.

None of this is to say that demography is destiny, or that
frustrations about job or life prospects necessarily translate
themselves into rebellion. A 2010 survey of youth around the
world found that Egyptian youths, for example, with all
their demographic baggage, ranked alongside their cohort in
Jordan, Vietnam, Indonesia, and Russia as the *least* likely to
participate in oppositional politics among youth populations
globally. As of 2004, Vietnam had a youth unemployment rate
of under 5 percent, and Russia a rapidly graying population—
very different profiles from that of Egypt. Furthermore, youth
was hardly the only segment of Arab populations that mobilized during the uprisings. Nevertheless, by 2010 there was a
cohort of youth throughout the Arab world with grievances.
Under the proper circumstances, this cohort was available to
be mobilized for oppositional politics.

How did a food crisis make Arab states vulnerable to uprisings?

In January 2011, the Japanese investment bank Nomura compiled a list of the twenty-five countries that would be "crushed"
in a food crisis.[9] The Arab world was well represented on the
list: Tunisia came in at number eighteen, with Libya at sixteen,
Sudan at eight, Egypt at six, Lebanon at five, Algeria at three,
and Morocco at two. To understand the full effects of these

numbers, consider that the portion of household spending that went to pay for food in the countries on the list ranges from an average of 34 percent in Lebanon to an average of 63 percent in Morocco. The average percentage of household spending that goes to pay for food in the United States is about 7 percent— a figure that includes eating as entertainment, that is, dining outside the home.

There are two main reasons for the vulnerability of states in the Arab world to a food crisis. First, even though the region contains two areas that have historically been associated with agricultural plenty—"Mesopotamia," the territory between the Tigris and Euphrates rivers in Iraq, and the Nile valley in Egypt—agricultural conditions throughout much of the region are harsh, populations are rising, and water tables have diminished.

Only two countries in the Arab world had reached the level of food self-sufficiency before 2006: Syria and Saudi Arabia. Then four consecutive years of drought made Syria a food importer rather than the food exporter it had been. Investment in agriculture had enabled Saudi Arabia to become a food exporter, and for a brief period in the early 1990s Saudi Arabia was the world's sixth largest exporter of grain. After the outbreak of the Gulf War in 1991, however, the Saudi government began diverting much of the money it had spent to subsidize agriculture to military procurement. In 2008, the government abandoned its grain cultivation program entirely, and two years later it was contemplating building a new Red Sea port geared toward handling imports of wheat and barley. Now all Arab countries are net food importers, and Egypt is the world's largest importer of wheat.

The other factor that has contributed to making the region vulnerable to a food crisis is neoliberal economic policies. As governments strove to avoid intervening in markets to fix prices or manipulate the exchange rates of their currencies, populations had to face fluctuations in international food prices on their own. In addition, the neoliberal policies that compelled governments to abandon across-the-board subsidies on food and replace them with subsidies targeted to the very poor have diminished food security for a wide swath of the population. They have also fueled popular anger when food prices go up. In 2007, for example, when prices began to climb, bread riots spread throughout the region, from Morocco and Algeria to Yemen, Jordan, Lebanon, and Syria. Given a choice between facing the ire of their populations and the ire of the IMF, governments chose the latter and increased subsidies and raised public sector wages. Egypt alone spent $3 billion for subsidies on food.

The increase in the price of food that the region began experiencing in 2007 turned out not to be a fluke. Between 2007 and the beginning of 2011, the price of food doubled on international markets, and as of March 2011 food prices had risen for eight consecutive months. Economists have given a number of reasons for the price increases. There is the increased acreage American, European, and Brazilian farmers have given over to the production of biofuels. In the United States alone, more than one-quarter of the 2010 grain harvest went to biofuel. (Rather than offering Tunisians and Egyptians IMF and World Bank assistance to further neoliberal policies in their countries, which President Obama did in his May 2011 speech to the Arab world, he might have offered them a very different type of remedy to their plight: an end to federal subsidies for the cultivation of corn for biofuel in the United States.)   ·

Climate change, which has had its most dramatic effect on Russia in 2010, has also affected food prices. As a result of a heat wave, the Russian wheat harvest declined by 40 percent and Russia halted its grain exports. Russia had been Egypt's largest supplier of wheat.

In addition, some economists cite the changing patterns of consumption in emerging economies, particularly China. As the standard of living in China has risen, so has meat consumption. And although estimates of how many pounds of corn are required to produce one pound of beef vary widely, there is no denying that the production of more beef requires more corn.

Finally, economists cite the effects of dollar inflation on food prices. As in the case of all internationally traded commodities, the price of grain is denominated in dollars, and when the value of the dollar declined in the wake of the economic crisis of 2008 the price of grain rose.

Whatever the causes, however, the fact remains that at the point at which the uprisings began and spread throughout the Arab world, the question of the vulnerability of the region to such a crisis was no longer theoretical.

Why did populations wanting change in the Arab world have to take to the streets?

The first Arab uprising, which broke out in Tunisia, took place a little over two years after the onset of the economic crisis of 2008. The intervening period had not been a good one for governments throughout the world, which found themselves caught between bankers and economists recommending austerity on the one hand, and populations fearing the end of the welfare state they had come to know on the other.

As the Arab uprisings spread, populations in other regions continued to show their dissatisfaction with those who governed them. They voted out ruling parties in the United Kingdom, Greece, Ireland, Portugal, Spain, Iceland, Slovakia, Canada, The Netherlands, France, and Italy, among other countries. In the United States, elections first threw out a Republican president, then a Democratic congress. And throughout Europe protesters and rioters took to the streets to prevent governments from cutting workers' pay and unemployment benefits, increasing the retirement age and cutting pensions, and eliminating bonuses to families having children. Yet through it all, not one government was overthrown, nor were political institutions uprooted. Blame fell on politicians and parties and the policies they pushed.

Now turn to the Arab world, where political institutions are weak and the lines separating the ruler, the ruling party, and ruling institutions (from the party congresses and "parliaments" to the military and intelligence services) are often blurred, if they exist at all. In most cases, popular representatives cannot be turned out of office because there are no popular representatives. In those few cases where there are, their power is limited. This is why populations throughout the region took to the streets as their first option. This also explains why the most common slogan during the uprisings was "Down with the *nizam*" (regime, system, order), and not "Down with the government."

Can we pinpoint the factors that caused the uprisings?

Unilateral attempts by regimes to renegotiate ruling bargains, demographic challenges, a food crisis, and brittleness made autocracies in the Arab world vulnerable, but they did not cause the uprisings. To attribute the uprisings to these factors or to any others overlooks a key variable—the human element—that determines whether an uprising will or will not occur. It also makes it seem that once a set of conditions is met, people will automatically respond in determined ways.

In the past, for example, it was common for historians and political scientists to attempt to connect uprisings with changes in economic conditions. In some cases (as in the case of the French Revolution of 1789) they have tracked the increase in the price of bread during the years leading up to the revolution and argued that the increase led to (in other words, caused) the revolution. Others, demonstrating that you can argue almost anything in the social sciences and get away with it, have asserted just the opposite. Uprisings, they claim, take place when a sudden reversal disrupts a period of improving economic conditions, thereby frustrating popular expectations.

The problem with both theories is that they cannot explain the countless times in which conditions for an uprising are met but no uprising occurs. For example, Americans did not rebel after the onset of the Great Depression in 1929 when the economy suddenly collapsed; nor did they rebel in 1937 when the economy again took a sharp nosedive after years of recovery. Nor can the theories account for the timing of uprisings, except with the telltale sentence, "After X years of hunger (or repression, or corruption), the people had had enough." The problem is that unemployment and bread prices, for example, are objective categories that are quantifiable; the sense of deprivation or injustice—not to mention the compulsion to translate that sense into action—is not. To make matters even more unpredictable, people's sense of deprivation changes as circumstances unfold. Thus they might suddenly discover a cause worth fighting for once their neighbors have taken to the streets.

Then there is the role played by unexpected events that people might latch on to (or not) to reinterpret their circumstances in new ways. As we shall see, the unforeseen departure of the presidents of Tunisia and Egypt in the wake of popular protests changed the course of an ongoing protest movement in Yemen; troops firing on peaceful protesters in Bahrain revitalized that protest; and the arrest and torture of schoolchildren in a provincial city in Syria, followed by the murder of irate parents and their neighbors by security forces firing into a crowd, touched off a rebellion that no one had anticipated.

All this raises the issue of the predictability of uprisings in general and the predictability of the Arab uprisings in particular. Although many observers of the Arab world had turned their attention to the problem of why authoritarian regimes in the region seemed so durable, others predicted their demise. They pointed out the many problems, particularly economic, that Arab regimes faced and asserted that in a post–cold war world in which democracy and human rights had taken on a new lease on life, autocracies were just outmoded.

The problem with these predictions was that they rarely offered up a timetable for events, and none foresaw the type of popular movement that swept through the region. Instead of envisaging masses of demonstrators shouting "Peaceful, peaceful" and demanding democratic rights, those who claimed to foresee the demise of regimes in the Arab world predicted that Islamists or disgruntled members of the regime would supply the shock troops for rebellion. Their predictions were thus like the proverbial stopped clock that tells the right time twice a day—except you do not know when that is.

No one really predicted the uprisings, but then no one could have done so. All rebellions—the Arab uprisings included—are by their nature unpredictable, as are the courses they take.

What was the spark that ignited the Arab uprisings?

On December 17, 2010, a street vendor, Muhammad Bouazizi, set himself on fire in front of the local government building in Sidi Bouzid, a rural town in Tunisia. Earlier in the day, a policewoman had confiscated his wares and publicly humiliated him. He tried to complain at the local municipality, but to no avail.

The self-immolation touched off protests that reached Tunisia's capital by December 27. At first, President Zine al-Abidine Ben Ali, who had ruled for a quarter-century, tried to pacify the protesters. He promised three hundred thousand new jobs and new parliamentary elections. This did little to mollify them. On January 14, military and political leaders had enough, and with the army refusing to fire on the protesters Ben Ali fled the country, leaving it in the hands of a caretaker government.

The Tunisian uprising was the first in a series of cascading events that swept through the Arab world. About a week and a half after the departure of Ben Ali, young people, many of whom belonged to an organization called the

"April 6 Youth Movement," began their occupation of Tahrir Square in Cairo. The security forces and goons-for-hire failed to dislodge the protesters, and the army announced it would not fire on them. Strikes and antigovernment protests spread throughout Egypt. On February 11, the army took matters into its own hands. It deposed President Hosni Mubarak, who had ruled for thirty years, and established a new government under the Supreme Council of the Armed Forces.

Events in Tunisia and Egypt demonstrated that Tunisian-style protest movements were viable elsewhere, and protests similar to those that had taken place in Tunisia and Egypt broke out in other places in the Arab world. After Egypt, young people in Yemen consciously adopted the Tunisian and Egyptian style of protests. In Bahrain, Jordan, Saudi Arabia, and Morocco, kings who had presented themselves as "reformers" now faced demands for constitutional monarchies. Organizers called for a "Day of Rage" in Libya after the arrest of a prominent human rights lawyer who represented families of the twelve hundred "disappeared" political prisoners who had been murdered in cold blood in a single incident in 1996. The regime met the protests with violence, precipitating a civil war between regime loyalists and self-designated "revolutionaries." A month later, it was Syria's turn. Although protests in the capital of Damascus modeled on those that had brought down autocrats in Tunisia and Egypt failed to gain traction, protests erupted throughout the country in the wake of ruthless regime violence.

Where did the demand for human and democratic rights come from?

So far, I have identified four factors that made regimes in the Arab world vulnerable to the sort of protests and uprisings we have seen since December 2010: attempts by regimes to unilaterally renegotiate ruling bargains, demographic challenges, a food crisis, and regime brittleness. To this list we might add one other: the global diffusion of a distinct set of norms of human and democratic rights that took place over the course of the past forty years.

Historians debate the origins of the notion of human rights. Some go back to the "natural law philosophers" of the sixteenth through eighteenth centuries, others to the French Revolution. Regardless of when the notion first appeared, however, it is undeniable that during the 1970s the conception, enforcement, and status of human rights as a global norm underwent a revolutionary change.

Before the 1970s, for example, the phrase "human rights" conjured up a variety of associations: economic and social rights, championed by the Soviet Union and its allies; collective rights, such as the right to self-determination and the right to national development, championed by the colonized world; and individual civil, political, and personal rights, championed by the West. The Universal Declaration of Human Rights, adopted by the United Nations in 1948, included all of these rights and others—although it did manage to omit the right to participate in sports that was guaranteed to all citizens in the 2012 Egyptian constitution. Since the 1970s, the emphasis in international assemblies has definitively shifted to individual rights, and the international community has signed a number of treaties guaranteeing their fulfillment. It has also established enforcement mechanisms, such as the International Criminal Court, which was established in 2002 and which indicted Muammar Qaddafi of Libya for crimes against humanity. How and why did such changes occur?

During the 1970s, the United States and the Soviet Union adopted a policy of détente—that is, a cooling of tensions between the two superpowers. But during the same period, the United States confronted a new challenge, as the Third World asserted more control over raw materials produced there, induced an economic downturn in the West by hiking the price of oil, and demanded a greater say in running the world economy. The Third World demanded the right to intervene into the global free market to "distort" it in its favor in much the same manner each Third World state "distorted" its domestic market by applying politically motivated state controls.

To counter Third World economic demands, the United States promoted neoliberalism. But in addition to promoting an open economic market, the United States began promoting an open political market. It was only logical: An open economic market depends upon autonomous citizens who would be free to gather information, make decisions, and freely enter into voluntary associations with one another whether on the floor of a stock exchange or in a town meeting. In other words, equating human rights with individual rights minimized the Third World state's capacity to intervene into and regiment the lives of its citizens, thereby undercutting the foundation of that state—which was causing the United States all manner of grief—both economically and politically.

The rhetoric of individual human rights served other purposes for the United States as well. By redefining human rights as individual civil, political, and personal rights, the United States challenged the Third World's attempt to associate human rights with collective rights—the foundation upon which the Third World based its demands for a "more just" international economic order. Furthermore, it put Third World states, where individual human rights were rarely observed, on the defensive in international assemblies. Algerians might introduce the Palestinian question or Apartheid at every opportunity, but as the American representative to the United Nations put it, every time they did so he would bring up the question of whether Ahmed Ben Bella—Algeria's first president, who was overthrown in a coup d'état—was "still presumably rotting in an Algerian prison cell."[10]

The American government put human rights language into the Helsinki Accords of 1975, a treaty signed by states in North America and Europe that confirmed the inviolability of national boundaries in Europe. The United States added the language for reasons having to do with domestic politics: Opponents of the treaty in the United States Senate complained that by recognizing the status quo in Soviet-dominated Eastern Europe, the treaty gave the Soviets what they wanted and the United States got nothing in return. Whatever the motivation in adding the language, however, the accords established a precedent and gave human rights legal endorsement. Thereafter, the United States pushed for its distinctive interpretation of human rights in international conferences, with varying levels of sincerity. The United States also selectively placed economic sanctions on regimes, sometimes those on the right (Somoza-led Nicaragua during the Carter administration), sometimes those on the left (Sandinista-led Nicaragua during the Reagan administration). The United States also gave material and symbolic support to dissidents and nongovernmental organizations wherever it might underscore the difference between "free" peoples and "oppressed" ones—and where it was possible to do so without otherwise damaging US interests.

It was, of course, easy for the United States to condemn the inability of Soviet Jews to emigrate, the suppression of Polish trade unions, and the imprisonment of East bloc and Cuban dissidents. On the other hand, it was not so easy for the United States to apply pressure on its allies in the Arab world since so much—oil, Israel, shipping lanes, and the like—was at stake. Thus, the United States tended to turn a blind eye toward every fraudulent election, mock trial, and broken promise of reform. It even allowed the foxes to guard the chickenhouses by urging governments to establish official human rights councils to measure their governments' compliance with international standards. By 2008, such councils existed in nine Arab states and the Palestinian territories.

How did the demand for human rights and democracy strike roots in the Arab world?

Placing human rights in the text of the Helsinki Accords might have been a cynical gesture, but it had an unforeseen result. In various places in the East bloc, NGOs such as Charter 77 in Czechoslovakia and the Moscow Helsinki Watch Group in the Soviet Union sprang up to monitor their states' compliance with their international obligations. A similar phenomenon occurred in the Arab world where official human rights councils catalyzed the emergence of nongovernmental bodies that kept tabs on human rights abuses and made the discourse on rights part of a shared political vocabulary. The first such group, the Tunisian League for Human Rights, was founded in 1976—two years before the founding of Human Rights Watch. Since that time, human rights organizations have mushroomed throughout the region.

Beginning in the first years of the twenty-first century, Arab human rights organizations undertook a number of high-profile initiatives to promote human and democratic rights in the region. In 2004 representatives from fifty-two nongovernmental Arab human rights and pro-democracy organizations organized the Civil Forum in Beirut on the eve of an Arab League Summit. In its final communiqué, addressed to Arab heads of state, the representatives outlined demands for political change, ranging from ending torture and releasing political prisoners to devolving political power from bloated central governments to locally accountable councils. (For those who would attribute a starring role in the Arab drama to the United States, the declaration explicitly rejected meddlesome interference from abroad.) Feeling the heat, the Arab League adopted a revised version of its 1994 Arab Charter on Human Rights at its Tunis summit two months later, reaffirming the rights previously enumerated in the forum's communiqué.

Similar meetings of rights advocates in 2004 resulted in the Doha Declaration for Democracy and Reform, the Alexandria Charter, and the Sana Declaration, each expanding its predecessors' lists of enumerated rights as well as the purview of civil society groups.

There was an additional factor that encouraged the spread of global norms of democratic and human rights in the region. Before the uprisings, most analysts monitoring events in the Arab world looked to Islamic groups as the most likely source for change in the region. After the wave of Islamist violence of the 1980s—a wave that resulted in the brutal repression, and in some cases elimination, of Islamist groups throughout the region—many Islamists in nonviolent, mass-based organizations such as the Muslim Brotherhood of Egypt turned away from politics altogether or pledged to work within the system. During the ensuing decades, Islamist parties won elections or made significant inroads among voters throughout the region, from Algeria to Jordan.

A new generation of Islamist activists who began their political careers running for office in professional organizations that represented lawyers, journalists, engineers, and the like adapted to representative politics. Through their participation in these organizations they also engaged with a culture of middle class/entrepreneurial values that sustained an ethos of individual rights. They were very unlike their elders whose political careers began with conspiracies hatched in prison.

By running in elections, Islamist parties in effect put their seal of approval on the democratic process. They also were forced to restructure themselves in a manner more appropriate to appeal to the masses. For both these reasons they removed themselves from effective leadership of any movement that sought radical change through extralegal means.

How pervasive was the demand for human and democratic rights in the Arab world before the uprisings of 2010–11?

Lest it be thought that human rights and democratic governance did not attract widespread support, the numerous protests and uprisings that swept through the Arab world since the 1980s provide evidence to the contrary. Many of these protests and uprisings were cross-sectarian or nonsectarian and many included a broad coalition of Islamists, liberals, trade unionists, and leftists.

The demand for human rights, democratic governance, or both lay at the heart of the "Berber Spring" of 1980, the fight by Algeria's largest ethnic minority for their rights. Eight years later, the Algerian "Black October" riots led to the first democratic elections (subsequently overturned) in the Arab world. The Bahraini *intifada* (Arabic for "shaking off," now commonly used to mean rebellion) of 1994–99 began with a petition signed by one-tenth of Bahrain's inhabitants demanding an end to emergency rule, the restoration of rights revoked by that rule, release of political prisoners, pardons for political exiles, and the expansion of the franchise to women. Petitioners also demanded a restoration of the 1973 constitution, which provided for a parliament in which two-thirds of the members were elected.

The death of Syrian dictator Hafez al-Assad in 2000 spawned the rise of political salons throughout Syria. Participants in those salons expanded their movement through the circulation of the "Statement of the Ninety-nine," then the "Statement of a Thousand," which made many of the same demands made during the Bahraini intifada, along with multi-party elections and freedom of speech, assembly, and expression. Even after the "Damascus Spring" turned into the "Damascus Winter," aftershocks of the mobilization continued. Among those aftershocks was the Damascus Declaration Movement of 2005, which (initially) united the secular and religious opposition in a common demand for democratic rights.

These movements were only the tip of the iceberg. Kuwait experienced two "color revolutions"—a "Blue Revolution" from 2002 to 2005, which won for Kuwaiti women the right to vote, and an "Orange Revolution" in 2006 to promote electoral reform. A number of secular and Islamist Egyptians banded together in 2004 to form a group called "Kefaya" ("Enough"), which called on Mubarak to resign. In Morocco, popular agitation led to the establishment of the Equity and Reconciliation Commission in 2004 to investigate human rights abuses that had occurred during the previous thirty years—the "Years of Lead." Lebanese took to the streets in 2005 in the so-called Cedar Revolution, demanding the withdrawal of Syrian forces from that unfortunate country and parliamentary elections free from Syrian interference. In 2004, 2008, and 2010 Kurdish citizens protested for minority rights in Syria. And the list goes on.

This history of mass agitation for human and democratic rights that swept the region for thirty years once again raises the question of why no one saw the eruption of 2010–11 coming. The answer is probably that observers who were focused on the wars being waged between Arab regimes and their Islamist opponents viewed each protest as an anomaly, driven by local issues, and not part of a pattern or wave. With 20/20 hindsight, we now know better.

How appropriate is the word "wave" to describe the spread of protests throughout the Arab world in 2010–11?

It has become very common to describe what has been occurring in the Arab world in terms of a "wave of protests," a "revolutionary wave," or even a "pro-democracy wave." The use of the wave metaphor is not a new one; historians have written about the "revolutionary wave" that engulfed Europe in 1848 and the one that engulfed the world in 1968 so often that it has become a cliché. Similarly, political scientist Samuel

Huntington discussed three "waves of democratization" in a 1993 book: a nineteenth-century wave, a second wave that took place between 1945 and the 1960s and 1970s, and a third wave that began in the mid-1970s and continued through the 1990s.[11] Some observers cite events in the Arab world as evidence that this third wave has continued, while others view it as the beginning of a fourth wave.

It is important to remember that in all these contexts "wave" serves as a metaphor, and like any metaphor it has advantages and disadvantages. On the one hand, there is no denying that later Arab uprisings borrowed techniques of mobilization and even symbols from earlier ones. Town squares that became the sites of protest throughout the Arab world were renamed "Tahrir" square after the main site of protest in Cairo, and the habit of garnering enthusiasm and relaying marching orders by renaming days of the week "Day of Rage" or "Day of Steadfastness" also came from the Egyptian model. Then there is the highly touted use of social networking sites for the purpose of mobilization.

On the other hand, the use of the wave metaphor obscures the fact that goals and styles of the uprisings have varied widely from country to country. In terms of the former, some protests have demanded reform, others the overthrow of the regime. In terms of the latter, there have been times when protests were predominantly peaceful and other times when they took a violent turn. More important, however, the wave metaphor lends an air of inevitability to what has been taking place in the Arab world. It was not inevitable. There are places in the Arab world, for example, that have not been affected. Most significantly, however, the air of inevitability connoted by the wave metaphor makes us lose sight of the tens of thousands of individual decisions made by people who joined the uprisings, and it takes away from the heroism of those who got up in the morning and decided, "Today I am going to face the full power of the state."

Where did the phrase "Arab Spring" come from, and how appropriate is it to describe events in the Arab world?

Springtime has always been associated with renewal, so perhaps it was inevitable that the Arab uprisings would earn the title "Arab Spring." This is not the first time commentators have invoked the term *spring* to describe political events. The raft of revolutions that advocated liberalism and nationalism in Europe in 1848 earned the title "Springtime of Nations," and the brief period in 1968 when Czechoslovakia flirted with liberal reform before Soviet tanks crushed Czech aspirations will forever be the "Prague Spring."

Nor is this the first time commentators have invoked the phrase "Arab Spring." Conservative commentators used the phrase in 2005 to refer to events in the Arab world that occurred in the wake of (and, according to some, as a result of) the American invasion of Iraq in 2003 and the announcement of President George W. Bush's "freedom agenda." Included among those events were the overthrow of Saddam Hussein's government and the first real elections in Iraq's recent history and the Cedar Revolution in Lebanon. In addition, Saudi Arabia held municipal elections, women in Kuwait marched for the right to vote, and Hosni Mubarak pledged that there would be free presidential elections in Egypt.

Unfortunately, the fulfillment of the promise of that Arab Spring proved elusive. In 2006, sectarian violence raged in Iraq, and Lebanese politics became hopelessly stalemated. Although the first municipal elections were held in Saudi Arabia in 2005, the next round in 2009 was postponed. And, of course, Mubarak's pledge proved hollow. The only success story was women's suffrage in Kuwait, which, as we have seen, came about within the context of a series of Arab uprisings that might be traced back a quarter century. Considering the track record of that Arab Spring, why would anyone want to burden the Arab uprisings with this title?

There are three other reasons to discourage its use. First, it is calendrically inaccurate: Only one of the uprisings—the uprising in Syria—actually broke out in a month that is in spring, although it broke out before the actual arrival of that season. The others began in the dead of winter, a season hardly appropriate for an uplifting title. The second problem with the title "Arab Spring" is that it is misleading. Since spring is commonly associated with joy and renewal, the use of the term Arab Spring raised expectations so high that they were bound to be dashed—as can be seen from a seemingly endless stream of articles with titles like "Was the Arab Spring Worth it?," "The Year the Arab Spring Went Bad," and "How Syria Ruined the Arab Spring."[12] Finally, the term implies that the struggle for political, economic, and social rights in the Arab world might be contained within the span of a single season—one that began in December 2010. As we have seen, there are millions of Algerians, Bahrainis, Syrians, Kuwaitis, Egyptians, Moroccans, Lebanese, and others in the Arab world who would dispute that.

2

THE BEGINNING

TUNISIA AND EGYPT

What characteristics do Tunisia and Egypt hold in common?

At first glance, it would seem that no two countries in the Arab world differ from each other more than Tunisia and Egypt. Egypt is the Arab world's most populous country, with an official population of 85 million and an estimated population of up to 100 million (because of conscription, not all families register the births of their sons). Tunisia, on the other hand, has a population of about 10.9 million. There is no comparison in terms of surface area either: Egypt is six times larger. On the other hand, Tunisians, on average, are wealthier (their per capita income is almost twice as high as Egyptians'), and at the time of the uprising the World Bank classified more than 80 percent of the population as "middle class." In Egypt, by contrast, about 40 percent of the population lived on less than two dollars a day. Tunisia also is more urbanized (68 percent of the population as opposed to Egypt's 43 percent) and more European. The slogan Tunisians shouted at their president during the uprising was "Dégage!" ("Get out!" in French). Egyptians, on the other hand, shouted "Irhal!" ("Get out!"—this time in Arabic).

In spite of their differences, however, Tunisia and Egypt share a number of key characteristics. These characteristics have a bearing on both the origin and the evolution of the uprisings in the two countries. For example, Tunisia and Egypt are relatively homogeneous. Approximately 98 percent of the population of Tunisia is Sunni Arab. About 90 percent of the population of Egypt is as well (the remainder is mainly Coptic Christian). Because of the relative homogeneity of the two states, political activists could not attempt to seize control by appealing to their followers' sectarian loyalties, nor could rulers of either state attempt to garner support by claiming that if he fell, the sect to which he and the core of his supporters belonged would be endangered (as rulers in Syria and Bahrain have done).

In addition, although neoliberal economic policies affected all states in the Arab world, Tunisia and Egypt held a special place in the hearts of those advocating economic reform. Egypt was the site of the first test of neoliberalism in the region, and the president of the World Bank once hailed Tunisia as the "best student . . . in the region" when it came to economic restructuring.[1] In both states, application of neoliberal policies exacerbated the divide between rich and poor, creating tensions that played out during the uprisings. Here's how *The Economist* described the Egyptian scene in 2008:

> Today, 44 percent of Egyptians still count as poor or extremely poor, with some 2.6m people so destitute that their entire income cannot cover basic food needs, let alone other expenses. Yet ranks of private jets clutter Cairo's airport. The flower arrangements at a recent posh wedding, where whisky flowed and the gowns fluttered in from Paris and Milan, were reputed to have cost $60,000 in a country where the average wage is less than $100 a month.[2]

Neoliberalism in general and privatization in particular bred a new social class in Egypt, known as the "fat cats," or more colorfully "whales of the Nile"[3]—a small group of *über*-wealthy businessmen who live in gated communities on the edge of the desert, thus avoiding daily contact with the inhabitants of Cairo's slums.

Similarly, neoliberalism has exacerbated the traditional geographic divide in Tunisia that separates the relatively prosperous north and eastern coastline from the poorer inland region. The former area has benefited from an economy built on tourism; the latter, dependent in large measure on small-scale textile production and agriculture, has suffered as a result of the removal of protective trade barriers.

Critical for understanding the paths taken by the uprisings in both states is the fact that Tunisia and Egypt also share a history of state building that stretches back to the nineteenth century. This sets them apart from all other Arab states.

Although Tunisia and Egypt belonged to the Ottoman Empire until 1881 and 1914, respectively, both enjoyed a great deal of autonomy. To protect that autonomy, local rulers embraced methods of governance and governing institutions modeled on those of European states, figuring that their domains could thus acquire the strengths of European states. So they "modernized" their militaries, constructed infrastructure, and adopted legal codes based on those of Europe. When the French made Tunisia a protectorate in 1881, they did nothing to reverse the processes of centralization and development, and when the British occupied Egypt (which nevertheless remained part of the Ottoman Empire) they imposed additional institutions and structures that fostered both as well (albeit for their own purposes). The process of centralization and development continued in Tunisia after it won its independence from France in 1956, as it did in Egypt after Gamal Abd al-Nasser and the "Free Officers" seized control in 1952 (although Egypt had received "conditional" independence in 1922, the British retained control of key institutions).

This history of state building left a legacy in both states of strong national identities, administrative stability, and autocratic rule. Strong national identities fostered the sense of solidarity that was so apparent in the uprisings—a sense that gave meaning to the ubiquitous slogan that began "the people want. . . ." And unlike in Libya and Syria, for example, no one predicted that the uprisings might lead to the fragmentation of either state. Strong institutions, such as the army, did not splinter, while others, such as the judiciary and the security apparatus remained in place even after rulers left the scene. The endurance of this "deep state" ensured administrative continuity, but it also provided a home base for "regime remnants" opposed to the goals of the uprisings long after autocrats had left the scene.

How entrenched were the autocracies ruling Tunisia and Egypt?

Strongmen ruling for long stretches of time have controlled Tunisia and Egypt for well over half a century. At the time of the uprising, Tunisians had known only two presidents since independence: Habib Bourguiba, who ruled for thirty years (1957–1987), and Zine al-Abidine Ben Ali, who ruled for twenty-four (1987–2011). Since the 1952 Free Officers' coup in Egypt, from which Mubarak's regime directly descended, Egyptians had known only three presidents: Gamal Abd al-Nasser (1952–1970), Anwar al-Sadat (1970–1981), and Hosni Mubarak (1981–2011).

Bourguiba was the leader of the Tunisian independence movement. A year after Tunisia won its independence from France, he deposed its monarch and proclaimed Tunisia a republic. He won election as the first president of Tunisia in 1959, and then three times after that until he decided to do away with the façade of elections entirely. Thus, in 1974, he had the National Assembly amend the constitution to make him president for life. Unfortunately, that life lasted longer than Bourguiba's mental faculties. In 1987, Prime Minister Ben Ali, who had risen through the ranks of the military before starting his political career, had doctors proclaim Bourguiba mentally incompetent, and in accordance with the constitution he became president.

In some of his first acts, Ben Ali raised hopes of Tunisians by abolishing the presidency-for-life and having the constitution amended to limit to three the number of terms a president could serve in office. Another amendment mandated the president to be under seventy-five when he takes office. In 2002, he dashed those hopes by backing a phony referendum in which Tunisians repealed the amendments, making him eligible for more terms. Overall, he "won" reelection five times, garnering anywhere between 89 and 98 percent of the vote each time.

Like Bourguiba, Nasser abolished a monarchy to become Egypt's first president. The end of the monarchy brought Egypt's so-called liberal age to a close. During that era (1922–1952), Egypt had not only a king but a parliament in which seats were contested, political parties that competed with each other, and a press that was relatively free. It was hardly a golden age, unless one associates a golden age with plutocracy. Nevertheless, it was less despotic than what would succeed it and the population could enjoy a modicum of political freedom. Nasser did away with the trappings that characterized the liberal age, establishing one-man, one-party rule.

After Nasser's death, Sadat, the hand-picked vice president, became president. It is possible to glean Sadat's concept of democracy from a confrontation he once had with a foreign reporter. When the reporter asked him a question he did not like, Sadat snapped, "In other times I would have shot you, but it is democracy I am suffering from." When an Islamist assassinated Sadat in 1981, his vice president, Mubarak assumed the presidency. Like Nasser and Sadat, Mubarak came up through the military (in this case, the air force). He "won" the presidency three times. It was not all that difficult: the Egyptian constitution raised so many obstacles for candidates that he had few rivals. Before the uprising, Mubarak did promise that the 2011 elections would, however, be "freer" than those that had preceded it.

How did the regimes in Tunisia and Egypt attempt to control their populations?

In both Tunisia and Egypt, the state put in place an all-pervasive security apparatus to monitor, frighten, and repress the population. The term *security apparatus* covers a variety of formal and informal groups with overlapping and often ill-defined jurisdictions. For example, because Ben Ali was not satisfied with entrusting the entirety of his security needs to the minister of the interior and the military, he used his own "sovereignty fund" to set up a parallel security force over which he had direct control. Mubarak was even more ambitious when it came to his security forces: an estimated two million Egyptians participated at any given time in Egypt's security apparatus. They ran the gamut from ministry officials to agents in the field to hired thugs to common snitches. Some were attached to the interior ministry. Others, such as those in the Central Security Services, acted as Mubarak's private army. Then there were those in the Intelligence Services, a branch of the military. Each branch operated independently.

During the 1980s, government officials, members of the ruling party, and private businessmen began to outsource their security needs to local hoodlums, known among Egyptians as *baltagiya*. The term was originally a Turkish word meaning "hatchet man." The baltagiya were drug runners, common criminals, gang members, former prisoners, or unemployed or underemployed slum dwellers whom the government, politicians, and businessmen hired to terrorize neighborhoods and political opponents, break up demonstrations, bust strikes, and in general contribute to creating a menacing atmosphere to cow the population.

How widespread was corruption in Tunisia and Egypt?

In both Tunisia and Egypt, tales of corruption took on almost mythic proportions. The inhabitants of both are used to dealing with policemen and civil servants with their hands out (because salaries are low, bribery is effectively built into the economic system). But during the uprisings, protesters vented their rage on corruption at the top. Take, for example, the system of crony capitalism that neoliberal reform engendered. In both Tunisia and Egypt, privatization of government-owned assets fed the corruption; those who had connections with, for example, the ruling party, or more important the president's family, were most successful in acquiring public enterprises, usually at bargain-basement rates. Thus the story of privatization in Tunisia contains a hefty subplot involving the family of Ben Ali's wife, Leila Trabelsi, while that of privatization in Egypt revolves around Gamal Mubarak, Hosni Mubarak's son.

There was, however, more to corruption than that bred by privatization, and there was a reason one of the most popular chants among protesters in Tunisia was "No, no to the Trabelsis who looted the budget" (it sounds better in Arabic). Thanks to WikiLeaks, which obtained and posted on the web cables sent by the American ambassador to Tunisia, details of the doings of the former hairdresser-turned-first-lady, whom the press called "the Marie Antoinette of Tunisia," or the "Imelda Marcos of Tunisia" (after another profligate spender), are widely known. So are the doings of her kin, who are called "the Family," with all its mafia connotations, in the cables. "Seemingly half of the Tunisian business community can claim a Ben Ali connection through marriage, and many of these relations are reported to have made the most of their lineage," one cable, titled "Corruption in Tunisia: What's Yours Is Mine," reported.[4]

That cable and others describe boundless kleptomania and conspicuous consumption: the Trabelsi clan, for example, owned the only private radio station in the country, the largest airline, several hotel companies, extensive real estate holdings, car assembly plants, a for-profit school, etc., all of which they obtained through insider dealings, bribery, expropriation, and outright theft. Two members of the family stole the yacht of a prominent French businessman and had it repainted to avoid detection. Another bought 17 percent of the shares of a state bank scheduled for privatization, which enabled him to gain control since the government put only 35 percent of the bank's shares up for sale anyway. And the list goes on. Few were surprised, then, that when Leila Trabelsi fled the country she had $56 million in gold bullion stashed aboard her plane.

While less colorful, corruption among the ruling elite of Egypt was no less impressive. Although protesters chanted, "O Mubarak, tell us where you get $70 billion!" that figure was an exaggeration. Nevertheless, the American state department did estimate that over the course of his presidency Mubarak had managed to accumulate $2–3 billion—not a bad haul.

Even more serious than presidential theft was the nexus of party leadership, cabinet or parliamentary membership, and economic opportunity. Ahmad Ezz, who came to control 60 percent of the Egyptian steel industry, was a close friend of Gamal Mubarak, an "enforcer" for the official party, and a member of parliament who used his connections to become "the emperor of steel." After the uprising, Ezz was indicted for allegedly blocking a 2008 law that would have forced him to divest from his monopoly. Then there is a former minister of agriculture, Amin Abaza, whose company was the largest exporter of Egyptian cotton, and a former minister of tourism, Zuhair Garrana, whose holding company owned luxury hotels and cruise ships. This list, too, can go on. Like Ezz, many of those on it have been indicted, had their passports revoked, or both.

How did the Tunisian uprising catch fire?

Two rumors have dogged the story of Muhammad Bouazizi, the twenty-six-year-old produce vendor whose humiliation and self-immolation provided the spark for the Tunisian uprising. The first is that the policewoman who confiscated his wares slapped Bouazizi in the market in front of others. She may have, but she was later acquitted of all charges arising from the incident, including that one. The second is that Bouazizi was a university graduate. He was not. Whatever their validity, however, the rumors might seem true to many Tunisians because they reaffirm two features of daily life they confronted: the daily abuse of power by those who could lord it over their compatriots, and the lack of economic opportunities, particularly for educated youths. The lack of economic opportunities was acutely felt in Bouazizi's hometown of Sidi Bouzid, which had a 30 percent unemployment rate.

The events that took place between Bouazizi's suicide on December 17, 2010, and the departure of Tunisian president Ben Ali close to a month later are straightforward. The day after the suicide, a crowd made up of fellow vendors, youths, labor activists, lawyers, and even some politicians began demonstrating in front of the local municipal building. Some in the crowd videotaped the demonstrations and posted the videos on Facebook, where al-Jazeera picked them up and broadcast them back into Tunisia. When the government cut internet connections, demonstrators sent cell phone images directly to the satellite TV channel. About three weeks later, unemployed graduates and students in the nearby town of Thala clashed with police, who shot five of the protesters.

The first reaction of the government in Tunis to events was to offer both carrots and sticks. As the first carrot, Ben Ali promised the protesters fifty thousand new jobs, enough for only about a third of the estimated number of unemployed university graduates. Over the course of the uprising, he upped the ante by pledging parliamentary elections and an end to internet censorship, and by vowing that he would keep the constitutionally mandated age limit for president at seventy-five years, making him ineligible to run for another term. And as leaders of Egypt, Yemen, Bahrain and elsewhere would offer during subsequent uprisings, he proposed sitting down with the opposition and engaging in a "national dialogue" about the country's future. But, warning that protests were scaring off foreign investment and tourism, he ordered all schools and universities closed to prevent students from massing—in the process ensuring that a steady supply of students with time on their hands would feed the protests. He then dispatched security forces and the army to put down the uprising. In the first encounter with protesters, the army unit he dispatched refused to open fire.

A few days after the carnage at Thala, the uprising, which had previously been concerned primarily with economic demands, took a decidedly political turn. In the town of Kasserine in western Tunisia, where twenty-one died at the hands of government snipers, infuriated protesters turned their sights on those responsible, demanding the immediate departure of President Ben Ali. The stakes had risen dramatically and quickly. Fueled by new media (such as text messaging), old media (such as al-Jazeera), and word of mouth, the uprising spread throughout the country. When it reached Tunis on January 13, the chief of staff of the Tunisian armed forces told the army to stand down. Ben Ali fled to Saudi Arabia the next day (the role played by the army in his flight is still not clear). This was the first time in the modern history of the Arab world a popular uprising forced the ouster of a ruler.

Why didn't the Tunisian uprising take place earlier?

On March 3, 2010, a street vendor named Abdesslem Trimech set himself on fire in front of the office of the general secretary of Monastir, a town on the Tunisian coast. Earlier in the day, Trimech had gone to the municipal building to protest the revocation of his vending license. After being rebuffed, he left, then returned with a flammable liquid which he poured over himself. Then he lit his lighter. Trimech was thirty or thirty-one years old (like many of the details of this story, his age is disputed), the father of two children. He lingered for a week while angry residents of Monastir clashed with the police. Tens of thousands attended his funeral (one report puts the number at 50,000 in a town of 80,000), which turned into an angry anti-government demonstration. The proceedings were videotaped and posted on social media outlets. In all, Trimech's story closely resembles that of Bouazizi's, with one exception: The day after the funeral, life in the town returned to normal and few outside Monastir cared much if anything about the incident.

It was reported that between Trimech's suicide and Bouazizi's, seven Tunisians had committed suicide by burning themselves to death. One of them, Chams Eddine Heni, a thirty-one-year-old from Metlaoui in west/central Tunisia, did so less than a month before Bouazizi. He had quarreled with his father over money he needed in order to obtain travel documents to Italy so he might escape the grinding poverty of his hometown. So the question remains: Why the differing reactions to events that were fundamentally similar?

Some observers have cited the fact that Sidi Bouzid is significantly poorer than Monastir—but then again so is Metlaoui. Others claim that local leaders, like trade union representatives and leaders of professional associations, did not link Trimech's death to broader political and economic issues—although the slogans shouted by the crowds after his act and at his funeral, along with the attacks on symbols of authority, seem to challenge the idea that there was any need for them to have done so. Still others argue that there was one significant difference between Bouazizi's suicide and the others: His was not merely recorded on social media, but al-Jazeera ("old media") picked up those videos and rebroadcast them endlessly throughout Tunisia and the Arabic-speaking world. This increased the awareness—if not the significance—of that event.

While appealing in its simplicity this explanation, too, fails to convince. By tying the Tunisian uprising to television coverage, this explanation resembles those theories that would tie the French Revolution to a rise in bread prices. It's what historians call "mechanistic" because, between stimulus and response, it leaves no space for human choice. Second, as we shall see below, placing some technology at the center of our story denigrates the role of those who chose to place Bouazizi's tragic death in a political framework and to do something about it.

Finally, there is also a problem in framing the question in terms of why Trimech's and Heni's deaths did not result in uprisings while Bouazizi's death did. Uprisings such as the one Tunisia experienced in 2010 are exceptional, not commonplace, occurrences in world history. Their non-occurrence needs no explanation. The real mystery is why Tunisians and the rest of the Arab world reacted to the death of Bouazizi as they did.

Was the uprising in Egypt like that of Tunisia?

The Tunisian uprising left an immediate and powerful impression on many people in Egypt. More than a dozen Egyptians, for example, copied Muhammad Bouazizi's suicide-by-fire. More productively, the Tunisian uprising demonstrated to the disaffected in Egypt and elsewhere that broad-based movements, such as the one that brought down the Tunisian government, were viable.

Those who planned the January 25, 2011, protests in Cairo and other Egyptian cities, for example—the opening salvo of the Egyptian uprising—have attributed their tactics, principal slogan ("The regime must go"), and ultimate goal (realization of that slogan) to their counterparts in Tunisia. In fact, a number of those who organized the initial demonstrations in Egypt knew their counterparts in Tunisia and were similarly young and technology-savvy. Hence, the widespread use of social media in both uprisings.

But even when events spun out of their control, there were important aspects of the Egyptian uprising that closely resembled those of the Tunisian one. Among them was the way in which the uprising fed off spontaneity, its leaderlessness, its rapid spread, and its nonreligious and largely nonviolent orientation. Like protesters in Tunisia, those in Egypt linked demands for political rights with economic justice and thus linked youths and labor activists in a common cause. And as in the case of the Tunisian uprising, the military in Egypt played a pivotal role, ensuring the speedy departure of the ruler.

How did the initial phase of the Egyptian uprising play itself out?

There were several groups calling for protests on January 25. Perhaps most famous was a group of young activists known as the "April 6 Youth Movement" who had worked together in oppositional politics for three years. On the eve of the protests, one of the group's founders, Asmaa Mahfouz, posted a video in which she taunted, "I, a girl, am going down to Tahrir Square and I will stand alone . . . and I'll hold up a banner, perhaps [other] people will show some honor." Then there were the administrators of the Facebook page "We are all Khaled Said." Said (pronounced Sa-*eed*) was a twenty-eight-year-old owner of a small import-export business in Alexandria who, it is believed, videotaped two policemen splitting up cash and drugs they had confiscated in a drug deal. Said subsequently posted the video. For his audacity, the policemen beat him to death. Somehow, his supporters obtained and posted photos of his mangled, beaten face. By the time of the uprising, the page had 473,000 visitors, many of whom learned of the protests from it.

Often overlooked in accounts that glorified the role played by the first two groups were activists from the youth wings of the Muslim Brotherhood and various political parties, along with labor organizers. Their participation ensured the protests would have the backing of a broad coalition.

Organizers chose January 25 because it coincided with National Police Day—a newly proclaimed national holiday that celebrated its widely despised namesake. The irony was not lost on the organizers. It was for fear of being branded unpatriotic, however, that a number of organized political groupings, including the Muslim Brotherhood, chose not to participate.

In Cairo, the police stopped most of the demonstrators before they could converge on Tahrir Square, the site designated to be the epicenter of the protest. But because the police were so scattered, they were unable to stop one group that had rallied in a working-class neighborhood. By the time that group had reached the square, its ranks had swelled to thousands. Others joined the protesters while they marched to Tahrir Square or at the square, until they numbered an estimated ten thousand. Borrowing a slogan from Tunisia, the crowd chanted, "The people want the fall of the regime." Toward evening the police moved in and, after skirmishing with the protesters, fired tear gas and cleared most from the square.

Because most journalists in Egypt were based in Cairo, protests that occurred elsewhere were, by and large, consigned to the inner pages of newspapers or ignored entirely. This distorted the view of how the revolution unfolded. For example, on January 25 protesters held demonstrations in twelve of Egypt's twenty-seven provinces and in most of the principal cities of the country. Outside of Cairo, in cities such as Suez and Alexandria, protests were more violent. In the latter city, police reportedly killed three protesters. In the southern city of Asyut, riot police with batons attacked protesters. Even bedouin in the Sinai desert engaged in running firefights with police that lasted throughout the uprising.

Also outside of Cairo, the profile of the protesters differed from that of the young, English-speaking professionals interviewed on American news. In Alexandria, the residents of some of the poorest neighborhoods joined the protests. In Mahalla al-Kubra, the site of the Egypt Spinning and Weaving Plant—the largest manufacturing plant in the Middle East— workers dominated the protests. They had been engaged in labor actions since 2006, drawing the attention of some of the youthful organizers who forged an alliance with strikers two years later. This is how the April 6 Youth Movement had cut its teeth in organizing.

Having seen that the demand for the resignation of Mubarak resonated widely with Egyptians, organizers called for another round of protests to be held three days later. In Cairo, scattered crowds of protesters converged once again on Tahrir Square, battling police who fired tear gas and beat protesters with truncheons. Late in the day, as the tide of battle swung in favor of the protesters, Mubarak allegedly ordered his interior minister to authorize the police to use live ammunition. When the minister's deputy refused the order, Mubarak deployed the army. Furious that he had been pushed out of the loop, the interior minister ordered the police off the streets of Cairo, hours before the army arrived. This was all the time needed for protesters to take firm control of the square, which became the symbolic center of the Egyptian rebellion.

Some protesters stayed in the square for the remainder of the uprising. Others fanned out throughout the city, attacking the Ministry of Interior building and the state-run television station and setting offices of the ruling party—the National Democratic Party (NDP)—and police stations on fire. The NDP was widely hated, and not just because of its role in sham elections and parliamentary debates. It was Mubarak's lapdog, and rather than serving constituents it functioned more like a club whose board divided political and economic spoils among themselves. Similar scenes of destruction were repeated in Suez and other major cities. In Alexandria, protesters drove the police off the streets altogether and seized control of the city until the army restored government authority.

The events of January 28 might be seen as the beginning of the end for the Mubarak regime. Mubarak remained defiant, and, up until his vice president announced Mubarak's resignation, he vowed to remain in office. The government even brought in goons on horseback and camelback in an unsuccessful attempt to dislodge the protesters from Tahrir Square.

They might have succeeded, too, had it not been for the unheralded assistance of the "ultras"—soccer thugs—who enjoyed nothing more than a good rumble with the authorities.

Nevertheless, the army's announcement soon after taking control of the streets that it would not fire on the protesters ultimately tipped the balance in their favor. And just when it appeared that the protests might be running out of steam, they received a shot in the arm: Wael Ghonim, the founder of the Facebook page "We are all Khaled Said" (and, as American media constantly reminded their audience, an executive with Google) appeared on national television and gave an emotional interview about his kidnapping and imprisonment by the government ten days earlier. Ghonim's interview reanimated the protest movement. Two days later, tens of thousands of Egyptian workers went on strike demanding wage increases and Mubarak's resignation.

On February 11, Omar Suleiman, Mubarak's recently appointed vice president (and designated successor), appeared on television and read this statement: "Taking into consideration the difficult circumstances the country is going through, President Mohammed Hosni Mubarak has decided to leave the post of president of the republic and has tasked the Supreme Council of the Armed Forces to manage the state's affairs." The army had had enough.

What was the role of social media in the Tunisian and Egyptian uprisings?

It was not long after the outbreak of the Tunisian uprising that Western media began to call the event a "Twitter Revolution" or a "Facebook Revolution," after two types of social media that the protesters used (protesters used other forms of "new media," such as cell phones and blogs as well, but those did not seem to have the cachet of Twitter and Facebook). The terms were readily accessible to journalists: they had already dubbed the 1978–79 Iranian Revolution the "Cassette Tape Revolution" and the 1989 uprisings in the Seychelles, Eastern Europe, and Tiananmen Square "fax revolutions"—all because of the technologies that purportedly enabled them. Then there was the 1986 "People Power Revolution" in the Philippines, which had the dubious distinction of simultaneously earning the epithet "Fax Revolution" and "Xerox Revolution," a discrepancy based, one supposes, on the authors' product preference.

Since 2004, it had become commonplace to name uprisings such as those in Moldova, Ukraine, and Iran after social media because participants had used that technology for one purpose or another. And after the outbreak of the Egyptian uprising (a second Facebook Revolution in a month!), journalists decided to abandon another term they had applied to the Tunisian uprising: the first "WikiLeaks Revolution," a title they had adopted that overemphasized the role played by the leaked American cables about corruption in provoking the protests.

The debate about the importance of social media in the Tunisian and Egyptian uprisings has involved two opposing camps, one made up of cyberphiles and the other of cyberskeptics. The cyberphile arguments underscore the essential role technology played in creating a community of protest in cyberspace since real space was not available in Tunisia or Egypt for anti-regime activity. Although cyberphiles admit that some participants in this community acted as mere observers, they argue that others created and actively involved themselves in an alternative cyber-based political sphere that paralleled the grim political sphere in which they lived. Their participation in this alternative sphere transformed their subjectivity (consciousness) and created a culture of rebellion and a committed engagement with practical politics.

Cyberphiles also point to the rapid spread of social media in the region, which overwhelmed the ability of governments to respond effectively (between 2008 and 2010, Facebook memberships increased in the broader Middle East 360 percent to 3.5 million), and the calls made by Egyptian Facebook pages for the January 25 protests that initiated the uprising. As a matter of fact, the group behind one of those pages, the April 6 Youth Movement, got its name from its call for a general strike on that day in 2008 in support of workers at Mahalla al-Kubra. According to cyberphiles, the call was the first demonstration of the revolutionary potential of social media in mobilizing protest in Egypt.

As cyberskeptics like to point out, however, the general strike of 2008 was a failure, as have been other uprisings in which social media purportedly played a central role (Moldova and Iran, 2009). So much for the near-magical potential of social media. Furthermore, attributing the Tunisian and Egyptian uprisings to social media underplays the role of groups that participated in them but were not as young or tech-savvy, and therefore not as photogenic, as, for example, the articulate young people in Tahrir Square. In addition, cyberskeptics argue that only 20 percent of Egyptians have internet access (to which cyberphiles might answer that fewer than a thousand Parisians stormed the Bastille in 1789), and that the government had already shut down internet connections before the pivotal events of January 28 (to which cyberphiles might answer that by then the uprising had already reached critical mass).

The most convincing argument made by cyberskeptics, however, is that attributing the uprisings to social media transforms the true heroes of the uprisings—the participants—from protagonists into patsies who act not because they choose to but because they are somehow technologically compelled to. This was demonstrably false. According to the *Egypt Human Development Report* of 2010, there was no necessary link between internet usage and politics in Egypt before the uprising: 60 percent of youths on the internet spent their time chatting, 20 percent looked at pornography, 12 percent conducted business or research, and only 8 percent visited political sites.

The answer to the question about the importance of social media to the uprisings in Tunisia and Egypt probably lies between the positions staked out by the cyberphiles and cyberskeptics. Social media certainly played a role in the uprisings, but they did not *cause* the uprisings. Like the printing press and telegraph before them, social media performed two functions in the uprisings: they facilitated communication among the participants and would-be participants who elected to take part in the protests, and they broadened the range of tactical options (such as organizing demonstrations in "real time," for example) open to those participants.

Why did the Tahrir Square protesters and others adopt the tactic of nonviolent resistance?

Some of the most evocative images to come from the Egyptian uprising were of crowds of unarmed protesters standing toe-to-toe with army personnel or security forces chanting "Salmiyya, salmiyya!" ("Peaceful, peaceful"). Protesters reenacted this scene countless times as the uprisings spread throughout out the Arab world—but, alas, all too often without the same outcome. The tactic of peaceful resistance was a logical one: protesters could not come close to matching the government in firepower, unarmed protesters were less provocative than armed protesters, and violence proved to be ineffective when Islamist groups used it against the state in the 1980s. Most important, there was the success of groups committed to nonviolence in Tunisia, some of which had been collaborating with their Egyptian counterparts for several years.

But the choice of nonviolence had other sources as well. During the decade preceding the uprising of 2011, there were a number of protest movements in Egypt, many of which were nonviolent or predominantly nonviolent in nature. In 2000, Egyptians took to the streets in support of the second Palestinian uprising (intifada) against the Israeli occupation of the West Bank and Gaza Strip. They were backed by striking professionals, labor activists, and students. Egyptians returned to the streets in 2003 to protest the American invasion of Iraq (during which they occupied Tahrir Square chanting "The street is ours!"), and again in 2005 in support of judges who held a sit-down strike rather than certify the fraudulent results of a parliamentary election. As a matter of fact, between May and December 2005, the blogosphere reported twenty-four peaceful demonstrations in Cairo alone.

Perhaps the two most significant events that reinforced the tactic of nonviolent protest were the activities and example of Kefaya in 2004 and the failure of the 2008 strike in Mahalla al-Kubra. Organizers of Kefaya—a coalition of political currents ranging from nationalist to communist to Islamist that united around demands for electoral reform—founded the group shortly before the government held a referendum to confirm a fifth term for Mubarak. Kefaya was the first group ever to call for Mubarak's resignation. One of its tactics was nonviolence: At its first rally, for example, demonstrators held a silent vigil, some taping their mouths shut with yellow stickers marked with Kefaya's logo.

Besides the symbolic power of nonviolence, organizers of the 2011 Tahrir Square protests learned other techniques and strategies from Kefaya as well. For example, Kefaya defined itself as a loose movement rather than a tight party to ensure inclusiveness, used social media to organize demonstrations, mobilized in working-class neighborhoods to broaden the movement's base, and asserted popular control over public spaces by organizing "flash mobs" to take them over for demonstrations. That Kefaya's demands and tactics matched those used during the uprising is not surprising: Although Kefaya had faded years before the uprising, one of the founders of the April 6 Youth Movement had been a member of Kefaya's youth movement.

The 2008 strike in Mahalla al-Kubra, from which the April 6 Youth Movement emerged, had ended in violence, and police intervention crushed the general strike organizers had called. In the wake of the failed strikes, leaders of what would become the movement sought out tactical pointers from others involved in struggles against authoritarian regimes. One of them, Muhammad Adel, traveled to Belgrade, Yugoslavia. There he enrolled in a one-week training program directed by the Center for Applied Non-Violent Action and Strategies (CANVAS), an organization founded by the nonviolent youth movement Otpor (Serbian for "Resistance"), which had spearheaded the uprising that brought down Serbian strongman Slobodan Milosevic. Adel was not alone; other pro-democracy advocates from Ukraine, Georgia, Zimbabwe, and Burma, for example, also received training in nonviolent resistance through CANVAS.

In the wake of the success of the Tunisian uprising, the April 6 Youth Movement and allied organizations prepared for an uprising of their own, this time to be played by Otpor's rulebook. The tactics they employed were pure Otpor. For example, instead of attempting to organize a single march to Tahrir Square on January 25 that might easily be broken up by security forces (a "tactic of concentration"), they organized twenty-one separate marches from different locations. One march was kept secret from all but the small group of march organizers, who drifted into position in groups no larger than ten (a "tactic of dispersal"). The April 6 Youth Movement even adopted the symbol of Otpor—a clenched fist—for its logo.

What was the role of labor in the two uprisings?

In both Tunisia and Egypt, labor activism has a venerable history, has long overlapped with political activism, and increased during the years building up to the uprisings. It should be no surprise, then, that labor activists in both places would put their skills in service to the uprisings.

In Tunisia, organized labor was at the forefront of the independence struggle, and after independence the trade union federation (the Union Générale Tunisienne du Travail, or UGTT) was one of two pillars upon which the new state rested (the other being Bourguiba's Neo-Destour Party). As a matter of fact, soon after independence there was a brief period in which it was impossible to determine whether the UGTT would become an affiliate of the party or the other way round. Since then, the UGTT had a checkered relationship with the regime, sometimes serving as a lapdog, sometimes standing in opposition to the regime's policies, particularly when they affected the federation's members. In 1977, for example, the UGTT called the first general strike in Tunisia's post-independence history, and in the mid-1980s relations between the federation and the regime got so bad that the regime clamped down hard on its rival.

Not all the trade unions represented in the federation march to the same drummer, however, nor have workers necessarily been compliant with their leadership, particularly when that leadership has aligned itself with the regime at their expense. Perhaps the most glaring example of divergence was the popular rebellion against the government-owned Gafsa Phosphate Company, the UGTT "aristocracy" in Tunis, and the government, which broke out over a hiring dispute in Gafsa, a region on the Algerian border, in 2008.

Like events that would take place two years later, the rebellion took on a political as well as economic dimension (protesters reworked election posters proclaiming "Ben Ali 2009" to read "Ben Ali 2500"). And like the 2010 uprising, it spawned a wide coalition (unemployed university graduates, high school students, unemployed workers and their families) and took advantage of a variety of nonviolent and violent tactics (demonstrations, occupations and blockages of public spaces, sitdown and hunger strikes, and violence against police and political authorities). The main differences between the 2008 and 2010 uprisings, however, were that the Gafsa rebellion did not spread to other regions and that the army stood with the regime. The rebellion was crushed, but in other ways foreshadowed what was yet to come.

Labor activism in Egypt dates back to the turn of the twentieth century. Most recently, there has been an upsurge in labor activism, particularly as the Mubarak regime pushed ahead with a neoliberal agenda. Workers have found privatization and attempts to hold down wages and cut back benefits in the midst of inflation particularly offensive. Most link privatization with reductions in a firm's workforce and cutbacks in benefits guaranteed by public firms. Between the seating of the "cabinet of businessmen" in 2004 and the outbreak of the uprising, there were more than three thousand labor actions involving more than two million workers and their families.

Labor activism spiked in the years 2006–2008, when it seemed that the entire textile industry and the communities that housed it had walked off the job and when the government was forced to recognize the first independent trade union since 1957. It would not be too far off the mark to say that labor activism became the primary form of resistance to the regime over the course of the decade that preceded the uprisings.

Labor thus came to play a key—and some would say pivotal—role in the Tunisian and Egyptian uprisings. In Tunisia, union activists exploited their talent for organizing early on to broaden the base of the protests, particularly among unemployed and underemployed youths. Professional associations (syndicates), such as those that represented lawyers and doctors, also joined the protests and were among the first to link economic grievances with political demands. Under mounting pressure from its rank and file, and with wildcat strikes breaking out throughout the country, the UGTT broke with the regime and threw its weight behind the uprising.

In Egypt, where protest leaders and the labor movement had an intertwined history, tens of thousands of workers from both the public and private sectors, including those from the petroleum, railroad, banking, retail, manufacturing, public transportation, health care, and heavy industry sectors, struck on February 9, 2011, and joined protesters on the streets of most major cities. In the volatile textile industry, eighteen thousand workers left their jobs, and walkouts shut down the Cairo airport and stock exchange. All this took place two days before the army told Mubarak he had to go. It might have been coincidence, or it might have been that the strike wave had demonstrated to the military that Mubarak's position was untenable. There is no doubt, however, that the military was watching the strikes with trepidation: a few days after Mubarak's departure, the military sent out a text message to millions of Egyptian cell phone users reading, "The Supreme Council of the Armed Forces urges honest citizens to take part in efforts to reach a safe haven"—a not-very-subtle demand for them to get back to work.

What was the role of Islamist groups in the two uprisings?

As in other parts of the Arab world, Tunisia and Egypt experienced a wave of Islamist violence in the 1980s that their rulers used as an excuse to justify repression and torture. In Tunisia, the government initially encouraged the Islamist movement, hoping it would serve as a counterweight to the UGTT. But when the Islamist party, Ennahda, demonstrated its popularity in the 1989 elections, the government clamped down hard, jailing members and driving its leader into exile. The party, which had vowed to work within the system, struck back with violence, calling for the overthrow of the government. Although the party was essentially destroyed in Tunisia, the government maintained its repressive apparatus even while much of the population became skeptical of its motives. Indeed, in the two decades preceding the uprising, the Tunisian government expanded and intensified repression to such an extent that Human Rights Watch declared Tunisia to be one of the most repressive states in the world—a world that, it should be remembered, includes Myanmar and Syria. It is partly for this reason that human rights became an issue of significance for Tunisians.

In Egypt, it was groups splintering off from the Egyptian Muslim Brotherhood or unaffiliated with the brotherhood that perpetrated the violence. The bloodletting climaxed with the 1997 massacre of sixty-three at the popular tourist destination of Luxor (the perpetrators wanted to bring down the Egyptian economy by targeting the lucrative tourism industry). As in Tunisia, the government responded to Islamist violence with heavy-handed repression. In the wake of the assassination of President Anwar al-Sadat, for example, the Egyptian government imposed an emergency law that entitled the state to restrict freedom of assembly, arrest and detain suspects without warrant, monitor and censor publications, establish exceptional courts to try those accused of violating presidential decrees, etc. Ending the state of emergency, which the government had once again extended for another two years in 2010, was one of the central demands of the protesters.

Although Ennahda received more than 40 percent of the vote in the election for the assembly charged with drafting Tunisia's post-uprising constitution, it did not guide or even participate in the uprising there. Such was the effectiveness of Ben Ali's repression. (The speed with which Ennahda regrouped after Ben Ali left, however, demonstrates it had not lost its appeal.) This was not the case in Egypt. In spite of the fact that the Egyptian Muslim Brotherhood officially refused to sanction the January 25 protest, members of the group's youth wing participated in its organization and played an important role in the uprising thereafter. After its late start, the Muslim Brotherhood did endorse the second round of protests on January 28.

In February 2011, the brotherhood declared that it would not back a candidate for president and would back candidates for only one-third of the seats in parliament in Egypt's first post-uprising elections (the brotherhood itself did not run a slate of candidates for office; rather, it established a political party, the Freedom and Justice Party [FJP], which did). Apparently, the opportunity presented by being the most identifiable and organizationally skillful association on the Egyptian political scene prompted the brotherhood to abandon this policy. In January 2012, FJP candidates won 47.2 percent of the seats in the Egyptian parliament, and seven months later the FJP's Muhammad Morsi won election as Egypt's first post-Mubarak president.

What was the Egyptian Muslim Brotherhood?

The Egyptian Muslim Brotherhood was founded in 1928 by a charismatic school teacher, Hassan al-Banna, to promote personal piety, charitable acts, and a Muslim revival to counter what many Egyptians believed to be a Western cultural onslaught. It was officially disbanded by a military-backed government that seized power in 2013 after it had reached the pinnacle of power in Egypt and performed in a manner that was widely derided by Egyptians. While the military-backed government condemned the brotherhood as a terrorist organization, its last confirmed use of violence was in 1948, when its "secret apparatus" assassinated the Egyptian prime minister who had ordered the organization dissolved (Nasser accused the brotherhood of attempting to assassinate him in 1954, but this might have been a ploy to give him license to crush his rival).

Since that time, some within the brotherhood have periodically become radicalized (mainly in prison) and left the brotherhood to form their own organizations, while others acted as if they believed discretion to be the better part of valor. After years of repression, the "general guide" of the brotherhood renounced violence altogether in 1969 and 1972, and his successor renewed the pledge in 1987 in return for permission to form a party so that the brotherhood might legally participate in the political process, such as it was. That permission was not forthcoming, but the organization did support candidates for parliament. In 2005, brotherhood-affiliated candidates won 20 percent of parliamentary seats. The government's response was massive electoral fraud in the parliamentary elections of 2010, which fed opposition to the regime.

Political scientist Carrie Rosefsky Wickham identified three currents within the Egyptian Muslim Brotherhood during the Mubarak and early post-Mubarak era.[5] The first consisted of those who foreswore political activity altogether in favor of preaching and pious activities. Their attitude seems to have been that there is no point to imposing Islamic law over a society that is unprepared for and undeserving of it. The second faction, probably the largest, combined conservative religious views with political participation. They wanted to reassert Islamic law and what they considered to be Islamic values in the public sphere.

Finally, there were those who chose to participate in politics but whose Islam was more liberal. It was members of this wing of the brotherhood who called for reform of the brotherhood's authoritarian structure, worked side-by-side with secular colleagues since their Kefaya days, were adept at using social media, and were at the forefront of the uprising. While never more than a small fraction of the organization at the time of its disbandment, their participation in electoral activities on university campuses and in professional organizations (such as those that spoke for doctors, engineers, pharmacists, scientists, and lawyers) introduced them to the world of contested elections and representative politics and signaled the possibility of a secular liberal/liberal Islamist political bloc in the future.

What are salafis?

One of the big surprises to come out of the uprisings has been the rise to prominence of salafi groups throughout the region, particularly in Egypt, Tunisia, and Libya. Salafism refers to a method some Muslims use for uncovering religious truth. The words "salafi" and "salafism" come from the Arabic phrase *"al-salaf al-salih"*—the pious ancestors—meaning the companions of the prophet who formed the original Islamic community in Medina under the guidance of Muhammad. Salafis look to that community as a model community. They also regard only two religious sources as valid—the Qur'an and *hadith* (reports of the sayings and activities of the prophet and his companions).

Because salafism is only a technique, the truth salafis uncover varies from salafi to salafi. Some salafis believe that Muhammad and the first Islamic community anticipated such contemporary ideas as democracy, women's rights, and the like. As it is most commonly used today, however, the term "salafism" refers to the beliefs and practices of ultra-orthodox Muslims who take a conservative approach to such issues as attire (beards for men, veils for women), women's roles, and minority rights, and stress the central importance of Islamic law and personal piety.

Before the uprisings, most salafis abstained from politics, arguing that so long as a ruler is a Muslim, it is sinful to rebel against him. Since the uprisings, however, three strands of salafism have come to the fore. The first, "scriptural salafism," continues the tradition of nonparticipation in politics to such an extent that prominent leaders of this tendency condemned the Tahrir Square protests and urged Egyptians to stand behind Mubarak. A second strand is more pragmatic, seizing the opportunities created by the uprisings to abandon their disdain for politics and enter the political fray. They formed parties in Egypt (the most popular being al-Nour) and Tunisia—and in the first parliamentary elections in Egypt stunned everyone by winning a quarter of the seats.

The pragmatic strand sees itself as a conservative counterweight to the more mainstream Muslim Brotherhood or Ennahda, and even though some within this grouping have been responsible for ugly incidents of mob violence

against unveiled women and members of religious minorities, attacks on churches, and skirmishes with their leftist
opponents on college campuses, others have been willing
to cast ideology aside—at least for a while. Thus, al-Nour
toned down its call for the immediate imposition of Islamic
law, put women on its electoral list (as all parties had to do)
and put their pictures on their campaign literature, pledged
to protect the rights of minorities within a civil state, and
even promised to maintain Egypt's treaty with Israel. Just
how far this twig can bend without snapping remains to be
seen (although al-Nour did stand with the military when it
deposed Muhammad Morsi).

The final strand of salafism to come to the fore after the
outbreak of the uprisings is jihadi salafism. One of the most
prominent jihadi-salafi groups is the Tunisian Ansar al-Sharia
(Partisans of Islamic Law), directed by an Afghan war veteran
and the founder of the Tunisian Combat Group, which waged
a violent campaign against the Tunisian government beginning in 2000. Jihadi salafists abhor the opportunism of their
pragmatic counterparts. They believe democracy to be a sham,
groups like Ennahda to be sellouts, and the establishment of
a civil state as opposed to a state governed by Islamic law to
be a travesty. They are confrontational, attacking liquor stores
and "unIslamic" cultural events, and engaging in street fights
with political opponents. And by committing high-profile acts
of violence—including the attack on the US embassy in Tunis
in September 2012, clashes with the military, and (allegedly)
the assassination of two opposition members of parliament—
they have proven to be the most serious destabilizing force in
Tunisian politics.

Why did the armies in Tunisia and Egypt refuse to put down the initial uprisings?

After the Tunisian protests reached Tunis, the chief of staff of
the armed forces ordered the army not to fire on protesters,

forcing Ben Ali to flee. The Egyptian military went further: having decided that the army would not fire on the protesters, the Supreme Council of the Armed Forces staged a coup d'état. It deposed Mubarak and took over the government while protesters chanted, "The army and the people are one hand!" The army remained in charge of Egypt for about a year and a half. Why did the militaries act as they did?

In Tunisia, the military has historically been relatively small compared to militaries in the rest of the Arab world—about 36,000 officers and men at the time of the uprising. This was no accident: Tunisia did not win its independence by force of arms, as did Algeria, nor did the regime come to power as a result of a military coup, as the regime in Egypt had. Habib Bourguiba, a politician (not a soldier), negotiated independence from France on behalf of Tunisians. The Tunisian army was thus the product of independence, not the progenitor of independence. Bourguiba, not wishing to risk a coup, deliberately kept the army small and out of politics. Since Tunisia faced no real external threats, Bourguiba could follow this policy without risking the country's security.

Ben Ali maintained the policy of his predecessor in spite of the fact that he came from the army. Instead of depending on the army to ensure domestic peace, Ben Ali depended instead on security forces he controlled directly and indirectly. The fact that the military and the regime were separate entities, that conscripts reluctant to fire on their relatives and neighbors filled its ranks, and that there was in fact no love lost between the marginalized military and the regime made the chief of staff's decision that much easier.

The Egyptian military is the polar opposite of its Tunisian counterpart. It is huge: the army alone includes nine hundred thousand men (including reservists). Unlike the Tunisian military, it is battle-tested and even participated in the largest tank battle since World War II (the "Battle of the Chinese Farm" during the 1973 war with Israel). Furthermore, unlike the Tunisian military, it has been pampered financially, both by the Egyptian government and by the United States, which gave it $1.3 billion annually from 1979 to 2013. Finally, unlike the Tunisian military, the Egyptian military has historically been involved in politics: all three presidents of Egypt came from its ranks.

Nevertheless, it would be a mistake to overestimate the military's political involvement. Although all three presidents of Egypt were military men, the process of demilitarizing the government began as early as the Nasser years. This process accelerated under Sadat, who felt threatened by the military's opposition to his policies, particularly the peace with Israel, which put in question the military's very reason for being. In place of preparing for another round against Israel, Sadat gave the military a different reason for being: it became a major player in the Egyptian economy.

No one knows for sure the size of the military's economic involvement (it is a state secret). Economists estimate that the military controls anywhere from 5 to 40 percent of the economy, and according to the IMF the military oversees about half of all Egyptian manufacturing. The reason is that the military can beat out all competition: (conscript) labor is cheap, the military can guarantee a steady supply of raw materials (some of which it produces itself, some of which it has priority claim to), it has access to the highest levels of government, and it is after all heavily subsidized. Thus over time the military has become involved in everything from construction and manufacture of consumer durables (like washing machines and refrigerators) to defense production and dairy and poultry farming. In addition, since many military bases are on Egypt's coasts and along the Nile, the military has had access to prime real estate ripe for development. And develop it it has.

The military's involvement in the economy, of course, violates the fundamental principles of neoliberalism, and some observers have noted the tension between the interests of military men and the crony capitalists around Gamal Mubarak who benefited from economic reform. As a matter of fact, this may have been one of the reasons the military was not particularly distressed to see the Mubaraks go, and why it immediately began rounding up the "whales" once they did. But there were other reasons as well for the military to push Mubarak out: it had a good thing going, and rather than see Mubarak take it all down, military leaders were more than willing to sacrifice the man at the top.

Why did the paths taken by the Tunisian and Egyptian uprisings diverge?

During their initial phases, the Tunisian and Egyptian uprisings bore a strong resemblance to each other. In both, mass protests forced the hands of militaries to compel autocrats to step down. In both, relatively free elections brought to power Islamist parties that pledged to play by the rules of the game. And both took place against the backdrop of state institutions that had evolved over centuries, providing continuity during difficult periods of transition. But over time the two uprisings ceased to move in tandem. Although dogged by constitutional crises, political violence, and economic distress, three years after the outbreak of their uprising Tunisians could look to their political future with cautious optimism. On the other hand, all Egyptians had to show for their efforts was harsh repression, another president from the military, and intense political polarization. Why, then, did the paths taken by the two uprisings diverge so dramatically?

Although it would be easy to attribute the different courses taken by the uprisings to differences in "political culture" (whatever that means), there were a number of tangible factors that fostered the divergent paths. First, there were the decisions made by military leaders about their role once the former heads of state were gone. In

Tunisia, the small and professional military went back to its barracks having handed over power to a national unity government composed of representatives of opposition parties, activists, and members of the old ruling party. In Egypt, the Supreme Command of the Armed Forces (SCAF) held on to power.

Preferring stability to reform, Egypt's new rulers not only dragged their feet on some of the uprising's central demands (including prosecution of the Mubaraks and lifting the state of emergency), they took a confrontational stance toward workers who continued their strike wave as well as protesters who continued their demonstrations. Thus, when baltagiya once again attacked protesters, the military stood by or fired into the air to disperse those under attack. And on the eve of Egypt's first free presidential elections, SCAF issued decrees that gave itself executive power above that of the incoming president, control over the national budget, and immunity from any oversight.

A second reason the paths of the two uprisings differed had to do with contrasting survival strategies adopted by the deep state in each country. When new rulers in Egypt attempted to effect change, the deep state acted as a brake. In Tunisia, it instead assumed the role of cruise control.

In June 2012, for example, Egypt's Supreme Constitutional Court and Supreme Presidential Electoral Commission rejected some of the candidates running in the presidential election on "procedural" grounds and effectively shut down the new parliament for similar reasons. The Supreme Administrative Court dissolved the first Constituent Assembly, which was charged with drafting the new constitution, and was on the verge of dissolving a second one when President Morsi issued a decree placing his decisions over that of the judiciary.

The police and security forces also refused to adapt themselves to the new order, and human rights organizations regularly condemned their brutality against protesters. After more than seventy soccer fans died in a riot at a match in Port Said in February 2012, prosecutors filed charges against the local police chief and others, alleging that they knew violence was likely and did nothing to prevent it. Their motive? To exact revenge on the ultras who had protected the protesters from the police and government-backed goons during the uprising.

In Tunisia, widespread street protests that continued even after Ben Ali fled demonstrated to authorities that Egyptian-style tactics would only strengthen the protest movement. When Ben Ali's prime minister stepped in to fill the deposed dictator's shoes, intense protests forced him out and the new acting president settled on a less provocative substitute, Béji Caïd Essebsi. Essebsi, too, had been part of the Ben Ali regime, but had a reputation as someone who had tried to rein in its excesses. As prime minister he performed a delicate balancing act, attempting to appease protesters when he could do so without provoking reaction from the deep state.

Essebsi dissolved the former ruling party (which had been nothing more than an empty shell anyway), dismissed (but did not indict) scores of officials close to the old regime, seized the assets of more than one hundred members of the Ben Ali-Trabelsi clan and their associates, and even oversaw the sentencing of the former president and his wife to prison terms of thirty-five years for theft (while doing nothing to extradite them so they might face their punishment). He dismissed a number of high-profile members of the old regime, but kept the judicial infrastructure intact. And when he left the government he founded Nida Tounis (the Call of Tunisia), an opposition party that came to represent not only secularists of all stripes who distrusted Ennahda but also offered political representation to the deep state.

The UGTT also remained intact and managed to maneuver itself into a position of mediating between Ennahda and Nida

Tounis when it appeared that negotiations over a new constitution had reached an impasse.

How did decisions made by governing parties in Egypt and Tunisia affect the course of uprisings there?

Different approaches taken toward governance by the Egyptian Muslim Brotherhood and Ennahda also contributed to the differing paths taken by the two uprisings. Muhammad Morsi, who assumed the presidency of Egypt in June 2012, was the brotherhood's second choice for president, the first having been eliminated by the Supreme Presidential Electoral Commission. Although head of the Freedom and Justice Party, he possessed limited political skills and horrified many Egyptians with his belligerent gaffes. He was certainly not in the same league as Rachid Ghannouchi, the leader of Ennahda, who had achieved global prominence while in exile in Britain for his work arguing for the compatibility of Islam and democracy.

But there was more to the different approaches taken toward governance than personal styles of the two movements' leaders. Although the Muslim Brotherhood had won only a plurality of seats in the Egyptian parliament, and although Morsi won a little over half the votes in a run-off election against Mubarak's last prime minister ("51 percent is not enough to rule," Ghannouchi warned him),[6] the brotherhood seemed to adopt the policy "to the victor go the spoils."

Neither Morsi nor his brotherhood colleagues attempted to reach out to the secular opposition (although brotherhood spokesmen said that they were the ones being shunned and not the other way round). Morsi appointed brotherhood members and cronies to key positions at all levels of government. When non-Islamist lawmakers boycotted parliament and the Constituent Assembly claiming the brotherhood had hijacked those two bodies and that their configuration violated the law—charges with which the courts agreed—Morsi not only ignored their complaints but rammed through a constitution in spite of the boycott. And when hundreds of thousands of protesters marched on the Presidential Palace to demand the postponement of the constitutional referendum, brotherhood goons attempted to disperse them violently, killing ten.

The behavior of Ennahda was a far cry from that of the Egyptian Muslim Brotherhood. After Tunisian voters gave Ennahda-backed candidates for parliament their plurality in October 2011, the party sought to establish a government of national unity and approached two secular parties, setting up what has been called a "troika," or government of three ("troika" is a Russian word for a team of three horses that pulls a sleigh). The prime minister came from Ennahda and the president and speaker of the assembly from its partners. This was an obvious attempt to allay the fears of non-Islamist Tunisians that Ennahda had a secret ambition to impose a radical Islamist agenda. It did not work, and as the secular opposition and deep state coalesced around Nida Tounis, as jihadi salafis grew bolder (killing a second parliamentarian in five months), and as the process of drafting a constitution deadlocked, it appeared that the Tunisian transition was in real danger.

Then the principal actors backed away from the precipice. To deal with its jihadi-salafi problem, the Ennahda-led government had Ansar al-Sharia declared a terrorist organization. Then Ghannouchi met with his principal rival, Béji Caïd Essebsi. After intense discussions, Ennahda agreed to dissolve its government and put the country in the hands of an interim cabinet of technocrats who would prepare for new elections. In other words, unlike their Egyptian colleagues who consistently worked to augment their power, Ennahda politicians voluntarily abdicated theirs. Finally, Ennahda parliamentarians endorsed the final draft of a constitution that repudiated much of what they had brought to the table (such as any reference to Islamic law) and supported positions they had opposed (such as gender equality). In all, 200 of 216 parliamentarians voted to adopt the document, which is now law.

There was another factor which drove Ennahda to reach a compromise on the constitution and seek collaboration with their political opponents: the example of Egypt. Tunisian politicians watched developments in Egypt with horror, from the polarization of politics into Islamist and anti-Islamist camps to the routinization of violence to the military takeover that derailed the Egyptian uprising, perhaps permanently. Unlike 2011, it was now the turn of Tunisians to observe developments in Egypt and weigh alternative futures.

Why did the Egyptian military overthrow the Muslim Brotherhood government?

The military coup d'état that took place in Egypt on July 3, 2013, was the culmination of a struggle between the Muslim Brotherhood and the deep state that had begun even before Morsi took office.

In the immediate aftermath of Mubarak's departure, the military and its allies undertook a series of measures intended to ensure that they would continue to play a central role in governance and that the Islamists would not rule, no matter how many elections they might win. Thus, the military claimed preeminent executive and legislative power, the judiciary and electoral commission disallowed several presidential candidates, and the judiciary dissolved the lower house of parliament and suspended the upper house on technical grounds. It also ordered the Constituent Assembly, tasked with writing a new constitution and chosen from the two houses of parliament, dissolved.

Upon taking office, therefore, Morsi saw himself and the Muslim Brotherhood on the defensive and believed, like the military and its allies, that they were involved in a zero-sum struggle with their opponents in which a victory for one meant defeat for the other. Over the course of the next year, that struggle escalated into a death match.

Although there was constant skirmishing between the two sides, three incidents in particular fed the escalating crisis. In the first, Morsi took on the military directly. In the wake of an attack on a border outpost by heavily armed militants which resulted in the deaths of sixteen border guards, Morsi forced the retirement of senior members of SCAF. He then promoted the youngest member of SCAF, Abd al-Fattah al-Sisi, whom Morsi believed he could control, to lead the council. He also ordered the end of the martial law regime that had sanctioned military supremacy and rescinded the SCAF decree that gave the military wide-ranging powers. In its place he issued a decree that expanded his executive authority, gave him full legislative authority in the absence of a sitting assembly, and authorized him to intervene in the process of drafting a new constitution. Although he would come to regret his promotion of al-Sisi, round one clearly went to Morsi.

In the second round, Morsi took on the judiciary. In September 2012, non-Islamists began boycotting the Constituent Assembly, claiming the brotherhood had stacked it with Islamists. Since the Supreme Constitutional Court had already ordered one Constituent Assembly dissolved, Morsi feared it would do so again in the wake of renewed legal challenges. On the eve of the court's ruling, Morsi did to the judiciary what he had earlier done to the military: He issued a decree that made his rulings—not the judiciary's—supreme and took away its power to dissolve the assembly. A week later the assembly finished its work and presented a widely criticized constitution for ratification.

Opponents of the constitution argued not only that the drafting process was flawed, but that the constitution was ambiguous when it came to such issues as human and women's rights, the role of Islamic law, and religious freedom. They also attributed clauses that allowed the military to remain virtually autonomous to a deal Morsi struck with the new members of SCAF in return for their cooperation in launching their palace coup against senior officers. Amidst widespread protests, voters approved the new constitution by a 62 percent margin in December 2012, with only about one-third of those registered bothering to vote.

The second round appeared to go to Morsi. He had neutralized the judiciary, placed himself above the law, and pushed through a constitution. But Morsi's victory proved illusory. Throughout the early months of 2013, the Morsi government lurched from one crisis to another. Protests against the constitutional process and the new constitution, sometimes deadly, brought out Egyptians *en masse*. The liberal opposition to the Muslim Brotherhood complained of a lack of power sharing and warned of creeping authoritarianism. But the real elephant in the room was the dismal state of the economy. By the spring of 2013 the Egyptian economy was in freefall. Foreign reserves had plummeted, the value of Egyptian currency declined 10 percent, and tourism—which before the uprising had contributed 11 percent to the national economy—had hit rock bottom. In May fuel shortages, which resulted in long lines at gasoline stations, electricity blackouts, and higher food prices, provoked widespread anger.

In April 2013 brotherhood opponents associated with the Tamarod (Rebellion) movement began a petition campaign calling for the recall of Morsi and early elections. Founded by five members of Kefaya, Tamarod claimed to have collected twenty-two million signatures on their petitions, although there was never any independent verification of this astonishing number. Nevertheless, polls indicated that by spring 2013 a majority of Egyptians disapproved of the job Morsi was doing, and on June 30—the anniversary of Morsi's accession to the presidency—hundreds of thousands of pro- and anti-Morsi Egyptians took to the streets. The following day the army issued an ultimatum that gave Morsi forty-eight hours to come up with a power-sharing plan or face military intervention. Backed by a coalition of anti-Morsi groups that ranged from the liberal opposition to the salafist al-Nour Party to former supporters of Mubarak, the military retook power.

General al-Sisi, who launched the coup d'état, became defense minister in the interim government, although he remained the power behind the throne. Adli Mansour, the former president of the Supreme Constitutional Court, assumed the position of acting president of Egypt and ordered the suspension of the 2012 constitution and the drafting of a new one, once again behind closed doors.

While the new constitution eliminated some of the oddities of the Muslim Brotherhood-backed constitution and enumerated lists of rights to which citizens are entitled (while stipulating that each right had to be exercised in accordance with the law), the big winners in the constitutional sweepstakes were the most important elements of the deep state. The military retained the autonomy it had won in the 2012 constitution. The judiciary, too, was freed from oversight and the Supreme Constitutional Court, which plays a role similar to the United States Supreme Court, won the right to choose its own members. And for the security services the constitution provided a Supreme Police Council which lawmakers would have to consult before passing legislation interfering in interior ministry affairs.

In January 2014, 98.1 percent of voters endorsed the new constitution, although once again only about one-third of eligible voters participated. Obviously, Egyptians were suffering from referendum fatigue. And, unsurprisingly, three months later General al-Sisi announced his retirement from the military and threw his hat into the ring as a presidential candidate. He won the post in May 2014. Although he garnered more than 95 percent of the vote (there was but one other candidate), turnout was an abysmal 47 percent.

Some might argue that the new constitution and al-Sisi's victory brought the revolution full circle. In January 2011, anti-authoritarian secularists and anti-authoritarian Islamists squared off against an autocrat and his supporters. By the summer of 2013, the political landscape had shifted completely. Rather than anti-authoritarian secularists and anti-authoritarian Islamists banding together against a common enemy, liberals and regime remnants, united by their hatred of brotherhood rule, joined forces in support of a new military-backed order. According to Tamarod founder Muhammad Haykal, "we succeeded in bringing back together these two populations: the foulouls [regime remnants] and the revolutionaries. . . . People are smart. They understood the real problem was the Muslim Brotherhood. With them, it's a cultural fight. They obey the brotherhood's values, whereas we obey Egypt's values."[7]

Do events in Egypt demonstrate that Islamist parties are incapable of rule?

It would be foolish to claim that events in Egypt prove Islamist parties in general and the Muslim Brotherhood in particular are incapable of good governance. All one has to do is look at the counterexample of Tunisia, where a governing Islamist party *has* reached out to its secular opposition, *has* participated with them in a national dialogue, *has* stepped aside when facing intractable political challenge, and *has* given its support to a draft constitution hailed by many observers as the most liberal in the Arab world. And for those who would blame Islamist failings elsewhere solely on the inexperience of parties which never had an opportunity to govern, it is important to remember that Ben Ali had destroyed Ennahda in Tunisia in 1991 and the organization had to be entirely rebuilt from the ground up in 2011.

Critics of Muslim Brotherhood rule in Egypt have accused the organization of hijacking the revolution by bringing two of its defining characteristics into the public arena. First, they point to its inclination for secrecy and subterfuge, through which it attempted to impose an unpopular Islamist agenda on the country. Second, they cite the brotherhood's own illiberal tendencies, derived both from its hierarchical and autocratic structure and from the nature of its ideology. As these accusations became increasingly widespread, they transformed the Egyptian political scene, resulting in extensive support for a coup d'état that overthrew a legally elected president. Events in Egypt in 2014 thus bear an eerie resemblance to events in Chile in 1973, where in the wake of an economic and political crisis the military deposed another legally elected president before launching a fearsome repression.

Any account of the tragic path taken by the Egyptian uprising must begin with an undeniable fact: Whatever its inclinations, the Muslim Brotherhood had first to wage a rearguard struggle against a permanent and unyielding state apparatus that sought, at best, to block its every move and, at worst, to force it from power. In the end, the brotherhood lost.

There were also a number of contingent factors that, when taken together, led to the decline in the brotherhood's popularity and support for a military takeover. To begin with, there was the incompetence of brotherhood rule, which was aggravated by sabotage committed by the deep state, particularly the judiciary and security services, and by Morsi's refusal to tap the expertise of those knowledgeable in governance. Then there were the personal inadequacies of the hopelessly unqualified Morsi. And as in contemporary Turkey and Russia, there was also the lack of constitutional impediments to Morsi's and the brotherhood's highhandedness that might have scaled back their ambitions and saved both from themselves.

One factor in particular encouraged the military to oust the brotherhood. Another built popular support for its actions. The mutually reinforcing institutional paranoia of the military and the brotherhood caused each to view the other as a threat to its very existence. As a result of this paranoia—justified though it might have been—the two most important political actors came to view Egyptian politics as that zero-sum game mentioned earlier which could only result in the destruction of one party or the other. And lurking in the background was the insoluble problem of the economy—its built-in deficiencies, its collapse during the uprising, the demands of international creditors for austerity and neoliberal reform in the face of popular demands for social justice—which will likely prove to be the Achilles' heel of all the uprisings and the ruin of revolutionaries of all ideological persuasions everywhere in the Arab world.

These factors, and not any inherent shortcoming of Islamist parties, were the reasons for the failure of Muslim Brotherhood rule.

What was political life in Egypt like after the military takeover?

Immediately after overthrowing Morsi, the military government of Egypt set out to eliminate the Muslim Brotherhood from Egyptian politics, exact revenge on its leaders, and cow its supporters. Then they turned their attention to the rest of the population.

The military demonstrated that it would brook no resistance, particularly if that resistance came from Muslim brothers. Within a week of seizing power, the armed forces killed fifty-one protesters who had gathered at a site where they believed Muhammad Morsi was being detained. Three weeks later, they stopped a protest march with lethal force, killing another seventy-two. And in the most violent incident of that bloody summer, armed forces raided and leveled two pro-Morsi encampments in Cairo. According to government sources, they killed 638 demonstrators and injured close to four thousand.

Sometimes, the vengeance meted out by the state boggles the imagination. In November 2013, a court sentenced twenty-one women, including seven under the age of eighteen, to prison terms of eleven years. They were members of a pro-Morsi group that called itself the "7 a.m. Movement" after the time of their planned protest. Although their demonstration was peaceful, they were convicted of belonging to a terrorist group and sabotage, among other charges. Then there was the bizarre trial that took place in Minya, a city south of Cairo. In two quick sessions, the court convicted 528 Morsi supporters of complicity in the killing of one policeman. Then the court sentenced all to death. Soon thereafter courts condemned another 683 to death for the killing of a policeman in nearby Adwa—including the general guide of the brotherhood. Lenin once said that the purpose of terrorism is to terrorize. That is undoubtedly the purpose of regime violence.

To prevent the possibility of organized resistance, the military government classified the Muslim Brotherhood as a terrorist organization and banned it, confiscated its assets, and arrested its leaders, including its general guide. They charged Muhammad Morsi with treason and with murder in connection to attacks on demonstrators protesting the constitutional referendum of December 2012. The government reinstated emergency law, restoring censorship, outlawing demonstrations, and allowing it to haul thousands of suspected brotherhood members and sympathizers before military courts, which the new constitution specifically enables.

And it is not just brotherhood members who are paying a high price for "anti-terrorism." In December 2013, a court condemned three secular activists, including two founders of the April 6 Youth Movement, to three years hard labor. Although convicted of holding an illegal demonstration, what they were involved in was far more dangerous for authorities. Their plan was to reanimate the movement that found expression in those eighteen days in Tahrir Square so that Egyptians might come to see that the military and the Muslim Brotherhood were not the only alternatives for their future.

How does the Egyptian uprising help us understand the other uprisings?

For many observers, the Egyptian uprising provides the gold standard according to which other uprisings should be appraised or viewed. For example, every year since 2011 the international media, along with Syrian opposition groups, have commemorated the anniversary of the outbreak of the Syrian uprising on March 15—the date in 2011 when a group modeled on the April 6 Youth Movement of Egypt held a demonstration in Damascus. Like its counterpart, the Syrian group consisted of educated youths who aspired to bring down the regime employing social media and nonviolent protest. Unlike its counterpart, however, its efforts were in vain. The demonstration brought together a minuscule number of protesters and was easily broken up by the security services. The actual Syrian uprising erupted on the spur of the moment four days later in two places far from Damascus. Unlike the Egyptian uprising, then, the Syrian uprising was spontaneous and lacked a core leadership that could define its goals and tactics—a state of affairs that goes a long way in explaining why the Syrian uprising became what it became. Using the Egyptian model to understand events in Syria leads us down a blind alley.

There are three factors that acted in combination to make the Egyptian uprising different from any other:

1. The Egyptian uprising never got a chance to play itself out. Like the uprising in Tunisia, it was interrupted by a military coup d'état.
2. Unlike any other state in the Arab world except Tunisia, Egypt possesses a permanent and unyielding state apparatus—a product of two hundred years of state-building. This apparatus—the deep state—proved impossible to dismantle with a single blow, as happened in other places. And it would continue to resist every effort at reform or restructuring.
3. In Egypt a popular mass-based Islamist opposition—the Muslim Brotherhood—was waiting in the wings. The Mubarak government tolerated the brotherhood so long as it did not overstep designated bounds. In most other

places, the Islamist opposition had either been obliterated during the anti-Islamist campaigns of the 1980s–1990s or was amalgamated with other opposition elements. Thus, in Egypt there was an organized, independent Islamist bloc that could and did co-opt anti-regime sentiment. As a result, what began as a secular/Islamist alliance against autocracy devolved into an Islamist/anti-Islamist struggle for power.

What are the five biggest myths about the Egyptian uprising?

After the dramatic downfall of Hosni Mubarak following eighteen days of protests, a number of myths have clouded the understanding of the initial phase of the Egyptian uprising in the popular imagination. Since those myths provide the lens through which many observers view the other uprisings, making them seem somehow substandard in comparison, it is time to put them to rest.

1. *Technology-savvy youths brought down Mubarak.* This is wrong on two counts. First, data collected after the fact indicate that 59 percent of Egyptian protesters were between the ages of 25 and 44—a rather expansive definition of "youth." Furthermore, as we have seen, in Egypt (as in Tunisia and Yemen) labor played a critical role— perhaps *the* critical role—in the uprising.
2. *The uprising proves the power of peaceful protest.* Not at all. As discussed above, violent incidents, ranging from street-battles to arson, accompanied the uprising throughout. Overall, the Egyptian newspaper *al-Masri al-Yawm* tallied about 850 fatalities and 6,000 injuries during those eighteen days.
3. *The army and the people were "one hand."* This popular slogan was more wishful thinking than a statement of fact. An official government report later charged the army with "disappearing" about 1,200 Egyptians—many

permanently—in the lead up to February 11. More were to follow in the following months.

4. *The uprising was all about human rights and an end to authoritarianism.* Again, this is not borne out by polling data. Nearly twice as many protesters cited the economy as a principal factor in their participation as cited their quest for civil and political rights. The ratio was even higher among protesters who cheered on the July 3, 2013, military coup d'état against the elected president, Muhammad Morsi.

5. *At least the uprising brought down Mubarak.* A military coup d'état, planned by the head of military intelligence, General Abd al-Fattah al-Sisi (!), brought Mubarak down. Elements within the military had been disaffected for years, believing Mubarak had side-lined what had once been a central pillar of the regime. The uprising provided them with the opportunity to redress their grievances.

3

UPRISINGS IN WEAK STATES

YEMEN AND LIBYA

What did the political systems of Yemen and Libya have in common before the uprisings?

In both Yemen and Libya, corrupt, aging despots who stifled civic and economic life lorded it over states they treated as their personal fiefdoms. As a matter of fact, Ali Abdullah Saleh of Yemen and Muammar Qaddafi of Libya were two of the three longest-ruling heads of state in the Arab world at the time of the uprisings (the third being Sultan Qaboos of Oman), and both intended to keep their posts in the family after they were gone.

What was political life in Yemen like before the uprising there?

Ali Abdullah Saleh became president of the Yemen Arab Republic (YAR, or "North Yemen") in 1978, when Yemen was still divided into two independent states, the YAR and the People's Democratic Republic of Yemen ("South Yemen"). At the time, the presidency of the YAR was literally a dead-end job: both of Saleh's predecessors had been assassinated, the latter by a suitcase bomb brought by an envoy from the South. Rumor has it that other than Saleh, no one wanted the job at the time. Saleh was a military officer who had had little formal education before entering the army. But he did have ambition.

Shortly after assuming control, parliament confirmed him as president. He ruled the YAR until the merger of the two Yemens in 1990, at which time he was elected the first president of the unified Republic of Yemen, a position he continued to hold for the next two decades.

Although Saleh was reelected president in 1999 with more than 91 percent of the vote (running against a weak candidate from his own party), observers considered the election to have been relatively free. It was thereafter that Saleh began to show his true colors. After announcing in 2005 that he would not contest the upcoming presidential elections to give a chance to a new generation, he changed his mind—bowing, as he claimed, to "popular will." Unsurprisingly, he won. In 2010, Yemen's parliament, which Saleh's party controlled, announced a plan to amend Yemen's constitution and eliminate presidential term limits, in effect making Saleh president-for-life. Only the uprising forced him to back down. And his plans went beyond the grave: he was grooming his son, Ali Ahmed Saleh, the commander of the Republican Guard and Special Forces, to succeed him. He had already begun shunting aside former allies and rivals—including prominent politicians, military officers, and tribal leaders—to make the transition smoother. This was one of the reasons many defected to the opposition when Saleh needed them most.

Ali Ahmed was not the only family member to benefit from his father's rule, nor were political and economic benefits restricted to family members alone. Corruption held the regime together and connected it to the broader society. Graft and bribery have been endemic to Yemen: auditors estimate that 30 percent of revenues do not make it into the government's coffers. Like other autocrats, Ali Abdullah Saleh peppered the security and military apparatus with relatives to ensure its loyalty. Such positions carry their own financial rewards in the form of kickbacks, access to government reserves of foreign exchange, smuggling and black marketeering of contraband, and the like.

Other relatives held prominent positions in government ministries dealing with planning and insurance and real estate regulation, while still others served on the boards of public enterprises begging to be looted, such as the national airline and the national petroleum company. Then there were relatives who used their access to enrich themselves in more traditional ways, such as through acquiring a monopoly over trade in tobacco, real estate speculation, and investing in hotels.

Outside the immediate family circle, Saleh regarded loyalty as a commodity to be purchased. And he was not the only one: the government of Saudi Arabia has regularly paid off Yemeni tribal leaders to keep their restive followers quiet (about the nature of the tribal systems in Yemen and Libya, and why they are not throwbacks to some earlier time, see below).

All this provided the context in which Yemeni politics played itself out, and no one with political or economic aspirations, either regime loyalist or regime opponent, could exempt themselves from it. For instance, the Saudis have paid tens of millions of dollars to the Ahmars, the leading family of the Hashid tribal confederation (a tribal confederation is a group of affiliated tribes). Because it is the leading family of one of the two largest tribal confederations in Yemen, and because Saleh is himself a member of one of the confederation's smaller tribes, he has also been solicitous of its support. The relationship was so close that the former patriarch of the family was called Saleh's "co-president." Members of the Ahmar family served the regime in the positions of speaker of parliament, vice speaker of parliament, head of the ruling party, and even presidential bodyguard.

One member of the family who has been the recipient of millions from the Saudis is Hamid al-Ahmar, a billionaire (who calls himself "the sheikh of Hashid Tribes Conglomerate"[1]) and former member of parliament. He thus had an insider's advantage when Yemen privatized its telecommunications industry. Acting in partnership with Orascom, an Egyptian communications firm, he built Yemen's largest cellular phone company. (The executive director of Orascom was a crony of Gamal Mubarak, the son of the former president.) Hamid al-Ahmar was also the leader of Yemen's largest opposition party, the Islah Party.

Islah is Arabic for "reform." Although led by a crony capitalist and associated with the Ahmar family, the quintessential political insiders, it wrapped itself in the mantle of Islamic virtue and presented itself as the "clean" Islamic alternative to Saleh's ruling party. Thus, even though the party opposed the idea of amending the constitution so that Saleh might run for a third term, it played the role of "loyal opposition" in a system from which its leaders benefited. It was thus slow to endorse the overthrow of the "nizam" (regime), as those who led the uprising demanded.

Making corruption all the more grating is Yemen's status as the poorest state in the Arab world, its 35 percent unemployment rate (at the time of the uprising) and 50 percent illiteracy rate, and an infrastructure that barely exists outside the major cities.

What was political life in Libya like before the uprising there?

Like Saleh, Muammar Qaddafi was a military man. In 1969, he led a group of "Free Officers" in a coup d'état that overthrew a monarch. If this seems reminiscent of events in Egypt, it is because Qaddafi modeled himself on Gamal Abd al-Nasser (in spite of the fact that two years before the coup the Israelis had demonstrated the hollowness of Nasser's pretensions to glory by routing the Egyptian army and occupying the Sinai in a mere six days). But after a short period of experimentation with Nasser-style institutions, Qaddafi concluded that Libya was no Egypt. He shifted course and imposed a regime whose chief characteristics were megalomania, repression, and corruption.

At times, Qaddafi's megalomania appeared farcical, as when he ordered soccer players to wear only their numbers on their jerseys, not their names, to prevent them from rivaling Qaddafi in popularity. In his attempt to don the mantle of Nasser, Qaddafi pursued Nasser's pan-Arab vision, and once it became clear that no Arab state took the vision as seriously as he did, he became champion of pan-African unity with Libya at the forefront, in the process demanding recognition as the "king of kings" of Africa. And instead of taking the title "president of Libya," Qaddafi adopted titles such as "Guide of the First of September Great Revolution of the Socialist People's Libyan Arab Jamahiriya" and "Brotherly Leader and Guide of the Revolution," so that he might appear more a philosopher king than a politician and so remain above the fray.

But this is where Qaddafi's megalomania became deadly serious. In 1977, he made his "Third Universal Theory," as presented in his *Green Book*, the foundation for remodeling the Libyan state, society, and economy. For Qaddafi, representative institutions were fraudulent, since the wealthy were bound to dominate them. What was needed, Qaddafi argued, was direct democracy. He therefore ordered the establishment of nested "people's congresses," which, he declared, would make direct democracy possible, and the dismantling of representative institutions. That is why by the time of the uprising there were no trade unions, political parties, or independent media in Libya. Likewise, he ordered the dismantling of economic structures that, he argued, would have created inequalities. Hence, no privately owned enterprises (or even independent grocery stores) were permitted. Libya was to be a *"jamahiriya"*—a term he coined to mean "rule by the masses."

Of course, since this system could not possibly work, government in Libya consisted of two layers: a formal layer of "people's" institutions, and an informal layer controlled by Qaddafi & Co. that actually did the governing. Rule by the masses was, in fact, an Orwellian nightmare. After the price of oil spiked in 1973 (and Libya is the largest oil producer in Africa), the influx of cash into Libya made it seem that the system was functional; the illusion was swept away with the collapse of oil prices in the 1980s.

Repression also kept the system going. Like many of his colleagues, Qaddafi employed multiple, overlapping security agencies, led by members of his extended family and close associates, many of whom he had known since childhood. But in addition to the usual agencies, Qaddafi took a page out of Mao's Cultural Revolution and established his own version of the Chinese Red Guards, the Revolutionary Committees Movement, which he entrusted to "safeguard the revolution." Members of the committees embedded themselves in every institution (even other security agencies) to ensure they maintained their commitment to the gospel of the *Green Book*, and, more important, that they not play host to anti-Qaddafi activity. The committees did more than just encourage right thinking, however; they also assassinated regime opponents wherever they might be found.

The security agencies established by Qaddafi won a well-deserved reputation for brutality. Examples of this brutality abound, but one incident in particular is significant for understanding the outbreak of the uprising. In 1996 the head of the Jamahiriya Security Organization, Abdullah al-Sanusi (who happened to be married to the sister of Qaddafi's wife), took charge of putting down a riot at the notorious Abu Salim prison in Tripoli. The rioters, many of whom had been jailed for belonging to the Islamist opposition to Qaddafi, took hostages, demanding better living conditions and the reinstatement of privileges that had been taken away. As negotiations between al-Sanusi and the prisoner representatives were taking place, guards herded the prisoners into courtyards. The guards then threw grenades and opened fire, and by the time the smoke had cleared about twelve hundred prisoners lay dead. The arrest of the lawyer representing the prisoners' families seeking information about their "disap-peared" relatives was the event that touched off the Libyan uprising of 2011.

Although the level of repression engineered by Qaddafi far exceeded the level even imagined by Saleh (until the outbreak of the uprising, that is), one would be hard-pressed to deter-mine in whose state corruption was worse. As in Yemen, cor-ruption in Libya was built into the system, in large measure because so much of the system depended on personal contacts and informal structures. According to a US state department cable released by WikiLeaks, "Libya is a kleptocracy in which the regime has a direct stake in anything worth buying, sell-ing or owning."[2]

Under the guise of "signing bonuses" or "consulting fees," Qaddafi, his family, and his associates shook down companies wishing to enter the Libyan market or expand their operations there; rumor had it that Qaddafi himself had to sign off on any contract worth more than $200 million. As in the case of Yemen, corruption was used to buy loyalty. Hence, Qaddafi set up foreign accounts for leaders of tribes loyal to the regime. And as in the case of Yemen, corruption simply flourished in an unregulated market in which members of the ruler's extended family could use their influence to ensure they got a cut of almost anything. It being Libya, competition among family members sometimes approached farce. In one instance, two of Qaddafi's sons engaged in an armed confrontation over control of a Coca-Cola bottling plant. It being Libya, however, the farce usually contained a strong dose of brutality.

Why do political scientists consider Yemen and Libya "weak states"?

The endurance of "strongmen" in Yemen and Libya seems to indicate that those states are strong. As a matter of fact, both Yemen and Libya have been poster children for a very differ-ent phenomenon: the weak-state syndrome.

According to political scientists, normal states exhibit three characteristics: a territory, a functioning government and bureaucracy that rules over the entirety of the territory, and a national identity. Weak states lack at least the second of those characteristics, and commonly the third as well. At the time of the uprisings government institutions were insubstantial in Yemen and Libya, and observers still contest the extent of national identity in both states.

Weak states survive only because of two factors. First, international law and international institutions guarantee their authority over a given territory, no matter how feeble that authority might be. Second, weak states adopt a common set of strategies to ensure their survival. Those strategies include winning the support of society's elites by granting them access to wealth and power, repressing the opposition, creating sham democratic institutions to act as a safety valve for political opponents, manipulating ethnic or geographic or religious divisions to prevent formation of a unified opposition, and outsourcing security functions to mercenaries or foreign governments to protect the regime without strengthening any groups or institutions. Ali Abdullah Saleh and Muammar Qaddafi used all of these strategies to maintain their power.

Four factors have contributed to state weakness in Yemen and Libya. The first is geography. Yemen's varied landscape, ranging from mountain to desert to canyon, makes it a difficult country to control, particularly since two-thirds of the population live in scattered and isolated villages beyond the reach of the state. Libya, on the other hand, is almost entirely desert, and although more than 85 percent of the population is urbanized and almost the entire population lives on a relatively small strip of land along the Mediterranean, that coast is long and huge stretches of desert separate the major population centers from one another.

The second factor contributing to state weakness is history. Unlike Tunisia and Egypt, which experienced two centuries of continuous institutional development over autonomous political communities, neither Yemen nor Libya had experienced either much institutional development or, until very recently, unity. The territory that is Yemen had been divided since the early nineteenth century into a "north" and a "south" (actually, a west and an east, but no one seemed to notice). Each political unit developed independently of the other. In the south, the British, who had taken the main port city, Aden, to use as a coaling station for ships en route to India during the nineteenth century, left behind a legacy typical of colonial outposts: a modern port, an active trade union movement, and politically savvy anti-imperialist schoolteachers, bureaucrats, journalists, and the like. After independence, some of their number would establish the only "people's democratic republic"—that is, a Marxist government—in the Arab world.

Little of this sort of thing took place in the north, where a Zaydi imam—the leader of a local Shi'i sect to which about 35–40 percent of all Yemenis still belong—established a kingdom with tribal assistance. Unification between north and south did not take place until 1990 and was not smooth, as the civil war of 1994 demonstrated.

Similarly, there was no unified Libya until 1934, when the Italians, who had begun colonizing the territory that is now Libya two decades before, united their three separate colonies into one. When the Allies pushed the Italians out of Libya in World War II, they could not agree on what to do with the territory, so they turned the question over to the United Nations for resolution. The result was the "United Kingdom of Libya," more united in word than deed, ruled by a descendant of a legendary anti-Italian resistance fighter who showed neither inclination nor talent for state building. During his reign, regional identities trumped the national identity, and even though a raft of ministries multiplied as the years went on, they functioned more as centers for redistributing revenues from Libya's newly tapped oil reserves than for actual planning and development—a practice continued by Qaddafi after he overthrew the monarchy in 1969.

This brings us to the third factor contributing to state weakness in Yemen and Libya: choices made by the leaders. We have already seen how this was done in both states. In the case of Yemen, what appears to be corruption to an unapprised observer is actually a deliberate attempt to incorporate family, friends, and potential rivals into the system to make them stakeholders. Formal institutions—whether a strong ruling party that exists for reasons other than to distribute patronage or a professional military that might become dangerous—would have diminished Saleh's flexibility to neutralize potential threats to his rule or absorb newcomers into the ranks of the elites. As a result, Saleh kept the role of formal institutions in governance to a minimum.

Similarly, Qaddafi created a cult around the lack of formal institutions within his jamahiriya—so much so that even one of his sons, in a rare moment of honesty, criticized the system his father built, blurting out, "We want to have an administrative, legal, and constitutional system once and for all, rather than change . . . every year."[3] It has been said about Libya that the only ministry that worked was the Ministry of Oil, which played an essential role in ensuring the steady flow of revenue from the state to the state's clients.

Oil is the final factor that has enabled Yemen and Libya to survive as weak states. Before the uprising, Libya acquired about 95 percent of its revenues from oil, which Saif al-Islam Qaddafi (Muammar's second son and, until the uprising, heir apparent) disbursed directly to loyal clients.

In the case of Yemen, the story is a bit more complex. At the time of the uprising, the Yemeni state derived about 75 percent of its revenues from oil, which it used in the same way Libya used its oil revenues. But Yemen's dependence on oil goes further: Yemen exports not only oil but labor to the oil-rich Gulf states as well. Yemeni guest workers then send home the bulk of their earnings to their families. These remittances, as they are called, are not negligible; from 2000 to 2007, Yemeni workers sent home about $10 billion, making Yemeni families the top recipients of remittances in the Middle East. Remittances take a financial burden off the Yemeni government by providing the population with an independent source of income, and they actually enrich the government as well: Yemenis buy foreign-produced goods with the money sent to them, and the government collects customs duties imposed on those goods.

Why is the fact that Yemen and Libya are weak states important for understanding the uprisings there?

Whatever the future might hold in Yemen and Libya, there was always one certainty about the outcome of the uprisings: they would not follow the same path as uprisings in Tunisia and Egypt. In the latter two countries, with their long history of state construction and institutional development, a functioning military stepped in to prevent complete elimination of the old regime by sending the most visible symbol of that regime—Ben Ali in the case of Tunisia, Mubarak in the case of Egypt—packing. This scenario was impossible in the cases of Yemen and Libya, because no unified and autonomous military, replete with a functioning chain of command and *esprit de corps*, existed in either. And although there was no institutionalized deep state to push back against the new regime as there was in Tunisia and Egypt, there was no functioning administrative apparatus either which would have made the post-uprising transition smoother.

What role have tribes played in Yemen and Libya?

Tribes consist of groups of individuals who are bound together by real or fictitious ties of kinship. Western media have focused a great deal of attention on the tribal system in Yemen and Libya, but much of their coverage is ill-informed. The common view of tribes in the Arab world is that they are exotic and archaic institutions. They are not, in spite of the fact that both Saleh and Qaddafi portrayed tribes as time-tested and fundamental building blocks of their societies in order to legitimate their method of rule.

The structure and role of tribes have changed as times have changed, and the tribal units that exist in the Arab world today are as much a part of modern political and social life as parties and trade unions. As a matter of fact, it is because of the weakness or absence of other institutions in Yemen and Libya—from government ministries to parties and trade unions—that the state turned to tribes to perform functions it could not otherwise carry out. The tribes of Yemen and Libya kept their members in line, dispensed patronage, adjudicated disputes, and, in the case of Yemen, got out the vote. The tribal system enabled regimes to bind influential tribal leaders to them, and tribal divisions were useful to the regimes as a means of dividing their populations and preventing the emergence of a unified opposition.

Although it is important to acknowledge the role tribes and tribal affiliation have played in Yemen and Libya, it is important not to overstate that role. Tribal leaders do not speak for the entirety of their tribe, and tribal members retain multiple other identities, such as regional or national identities, which often take precedence over their tribal identities. During the uprisings in both Yemen and Libya, tribes and tribal confederations even divided along political lines, with some members taking the side of the government and others the side of the opposition.

How did the uprising in Yemen evolve?

At the time of the uprising in Yemen there were two protest movements. One fostered the uprising, the other had a checkered history with it.

At the end of January 2011, a coalition of opposition parties called the Joint Meeting Parties (JMP) began a series of demonstrations in Yemen's capital, Sana, protesting the plan adopted by parliament to eliminate presidential term limits and Saleh's plan to have his son succeed him. This was the so-called Pink Revolution, named after the color they had chosen to identify their movement. It was led by political "outs" seeking "in," and their agenda was anything but the sort of regime change advocated by the protesters who had just brought down Ben Ali in Tunisia. Social networking youths similar to those who were leading protests in Egypt participated, but their role was peripheral—as was their call for Saleh to depart immediately.

By the first week in February 2011, Saleh had not only acceded to the political demands of the Pink Revolution, he made economic concessions as well, promising to create a fund to employ university graduates and to increase wages, among other initiatives. He also declared his willingness to resume the dialogue with the opposition that had collapsed months before. The Yemeni revolution appeared to be over before it had begun.

On February 11, the date of Egyptian president Mubarak's resignation, the JMP and the youths swapped roles. That night, students, youth activists, and others gathered outside Sana University. They marched to the city's main square, which, like its counterpart in Cairo, was named Tahrir Square, demanding the immediate resignation of Saleh. After a brief demonstration, security forces and "pro-regime demonstrators" (actually baltagiya—hoodlums employed by the government) forced them out and seized control of the square. The protesters returned to the university and set up camp in the square outside, renaming it "Taghayr [Change] Square." This would remain the epicenter of the rebellion in Sana as larger and larger numbers of demonstrators, inspired by events in Egypt and repelled by the violence the regime inflicted on protesters, joined them.

As in the case of Egypt, the world focused its attention on the capital city. But as in the case of Egypt, the capital was not the only city in which protests broke out. University students and workers in the city of Taiz (pronounced Ta-*iz*), south of

Sana, for example, also began their protests on February 11, and within a few days their numbers exceeded the numbers of those participating in marches in the capital. Likewise in the southern port city of Aden, where protesters advocating a restoration of South Yemeni independence joined others calling for the immediate departure of Saleh. And as in the case of Egypt, the level of violence outside the capital exceeded that within it—at least initially. During the first week of protests in Taiz, an unidentified government supporter threw a grenade into a crowd, killing two and injuring more than forty. In Aden, government snipers shot and killed eleven.

The regime in Yemen depended on the compliance, or at least the quiescence, of influential tribal, political, and military leaders whom it bought and balanced off against one another. As the protest movement broadened its base of support and spread throughout the country, and as the regime's resort to ever-increasing levels of violence provoked further resistance, those leaders smelled blood in the water and began to defect. First, members of the Ahmar family threw their support behind the protesters and flooded Sana with thousands of their followers. Then the JMP reversed itself and called for Saleh to leave immediately. After the massacre of forty-six protesters in Sana, a top military commander whom Saleh had given the thankless task of fighting a rebellion in the north followed suit and established a protective cordon around Taghrayr Square.

By the end of March 2011, Sana was a city divided between military units and armed supporters loyal to the regime and military units and armed supporters opposed to it. To break the stalemate, regime loyalists attacked the Sana compound of the Ahmar family. Although the attack failed, it sparked heavy fighting in the city. Soon thereafter, a bomb detonated in the presidential palace, killing eleven and severely wounding Saleh, who was evacuated to Saudi Arabia for medical treatment. He was treated and returned, but by that time the international community had had enough.

The United States, the Gulf Cooperation Council (GCC—the Saudi-dominated association of Gulf monarchies), and the United Nations brokered a deal: Saleh would step down as president and receive immunity, his vice president Abdu Rabbu Mansour Hadi would assume the post of acting president (he later ran unopposed for the post of president and, of course, won handily), and Yemen's fate would be placed in the hands of a National Dialogue Conference. This phase of the Yemeni uprising ended not so much with a bang but a whimper.

How did the uprising in Libya begin?

In the aftermath of the Tunisian and Egyptian uprisings, a coalition of groups issued a call on social media for Libyans to participate in their own Day of Rage to protest political and economic conditions in Libya. The date they chose was February 17, 2011. Events overtook the planned Day of Rage, however. On February 15, the Libyan government arrested Fathi Terbil, the lawyer representing the families of the "disappeared" prisoners of Abu Salim prison. Several hundred family members and their supporters gathered at the headquarters of a local Revolutionary Committee in Benghazi, then clashed with security forces. By the time the actual Day of Rage rolled around, six thousand protesters were in the streets of Benghazi calling for the overthrow of the regime, and protests and clashes had already spread to a number of towns surrounding Libya's second largest city, which protesters declared to be "liberated" from the regime.

It is not surprising that the uprising broke out in eastern Libya, where government control was less concentrated than in the west and where resentments about higher unemployment and lower government investment festered. But within days the uprising had spread west to Libya's capital, Tripoli, where protesters set fire to government buildings and engaged government forces in street battles, as well as to other cities and towns as far west as the Tunisian border. And as in Yemen, the lack of institutional development and formally established lines of authority resulted in a wave of defections from the regime, including ambassadors safely ensconced abroad, tribal leaders, and ranking military personnel who sometimes brought their units with them.

From the beginning, the regime met the uprising with an appalling level of violence. Security forces and the military treated the protesters as combatants: government forces forswore tear gas for live fire, and the government deployed helicopter gunships to put down the uprising in Tripoli. Elite units under the command of four of Qaddafi's seven sons remained loyal, of course, as did the twenty-five-hundred-man Islamic Pan-African Brigade, made up of fighters from Chad, Sudan, and Niger. Most of the air force, whose leaders were affiliated with Qaddafi's tribe, and the security forces, which consisted of members of Qaddafi's family and tribe and members of allied tribes, also remained loyal. Qaddafi had lavished his special units with military hardware while starving the regular army of resources to prevent a coup.

It is for this reason that even after foreign intervention, the uprising, which had already morphed into a civil war, settled into a protracted stalemate. It was only after six months of intense fighting, and the engagement of NATO jets providing close combat air support to the rebels, that the tide of battle turned. Tripoli fell to the rebels (who, in fact, referred to themselves as *thuwwar* [revolutionaries] to deny the Qaddafi regime any legitimacy) in August 2011. Two months later, they found and killed Qaddafi in his home town of Surt.

Was Qaddafi crazy, or crazy like a fox?

Besides excelling in megalomania, Muammar Qaddafi was also the Arab leader most likely to be characterized as "bizarre." After Swiss police arrested one of his sons, Hannibal (yes, Hannibal!), and his wife for beating two of their servants, the elder Qaddafi called for the abolition of Switzerland at the United Nations. He slept in a tent on state visits, introduced Italian prime minister Silvio Berlusconi to something called "bunga-bunga parties" (apparently, variations on more prosaic orgies), and surrounded himself with a special unit of all-female bodyguards known as Amazons. More seriously, he sponsored terrorist activities such as the downing of Pan Am flight 103 over Lockerbie, Scotland, which killed all 259 aboard and 11 on the ground. For acts such as these, President Ronald Reagan referred to Qaddafi as "the mad dog of the Middle East."

Although none of this seems like the actions of a sane man, there might have been method to Qaddafi's madness. In a state in which few formal institutions existed (even before the *Green Book*), charismatic leadership trumps bureaucratic stability. And there is no question that charisma was Qaddafi's strong suit, at least in his younger days. Furthermore, it might be argued that earning international opprobrium and even sanctions and supporting anti-imperialist revolutionaries everywhere had a domestic upside, inasmuch as it might have bonded a fractious population with one another and with their leader. Dueling with a superpower *mano a mano* certainly put a rather inconsequential country of 6.5 million people on the map, which might have been as much a source of pride for Libyans as a source of embarrassment. Finally, Qaddafi's buffoonish behavior shifted attention away from his regime's horrific human rights record—that is, until the uprising put that record in stark relief.

Why did the uprisings in Yemen and Libya turn violent?

Saif al-Islam Qaddafi blamed the violent nature of Libya's uprising on Libya's "tribal character." The highly respected

International Crisis Group cites infiltration of violent elements into the ranks of peaceful demonstrators in Benghazi. Still others have blamed the euphoria of the protesters after their initial successes and the looting of armories abandoned by government troops.[4] Yemen too is "tribal" (although this explanation rests on two dubious assumptions: that tribal affiliation and violence are necessarily linked, and that calling a society "tribal" actually tells you something meaningful about the society). Then there is the fact that Yemen has the most heavily armed population in the Arab world. It is, after all, a country in which carrying a ceremonial dagger is considered a fashion statement.

Lurking behind the question is the contrast between events as they purportedly unfolded in Tunisia and Egypt and events in Yemen and Libya. Although the nonviolence of the earlier uprisings has been overstated, there *is* an important contrast between Tunisia and Egypt on the one hand and Yemen and Libya on the other. The first two uprisings succeeded in dislodging autocrats because the army acted as a unit, declared *its* commitment to nonviolence, and in some cases even kept protesters and the thugs hired to attack them separated. Such was not the case in Yemen and Libya, where, rather than quashing the violence, militaries and a variety of other armed groups divided into loyalist and opposition camps. It was not that the protesters in Yemen and Libya weighed nonviolence against violence and found the former somehow wanting. Rather, the weakness of the two states and the fragmentation of the army—the very institution that had imposed order in Tunisia and Egypt—defined the tactics protesters had at their disposal.

Why did outside powers intervene in Libya?

It should not be surprising that the Europeans—particularly the French—and not the Americans led the charge for intervention in Libya on the side of the rebels. As a matter of fact, the Obama administration was widely ridiculed when an unnamed advisor told *The New Yorker* magazine that the United States would be "leading from behind" in Libya. Europe has greater interest in Libya for two reasons: oil and immigration. Before the uprising, the European Union imported about 10 percent of its oil from Libya (Italy was the largest market, importing about 25 percent of its oil from Libya). As for immigration, Europeans feared not only a massive wave from Libya if Qaddafi continued his violence but also a massive wave from sub-Saharan Africa if government control over Libya's coastline broke down.

With these issues in the background, there was another one that likely impelled the French to take the lead in pushing for international intervention: domestic politics. The government of French president Nicolas Sarkozy, the first to recognize the revolutionary government in Benghazi, was slow to support the uprising in Tunisia, a state in which France had a long-standing interest. Having missed the boat the first time, Sarkozy undoubtedly wanted to make sure he did not do so a second—particularly since he was entering an electoral campaign deeply unpopular and donning the mantle of Charles De Gaulle might just put him over the top. It didn't—France intervened under NATO auspices, but Sarkozy lost the presidency anyway.

For the United States, the stakes were different. As a matter of fact, since the United States had no real interests in Libya, the stakes were negligible. The United States had cut relations with Libya and imposed sanctions on the country in 1986 because of its sponsorship of terrorism. It removed sanctions in 2002 after Libya assumed legal and financial responsibility for its most outrageous terrorist acts and after Qaddafi renounced the pursuit of weapons of mass destruction. Although the United States once again began importing oil from Libya, Libyan oil accounted for only 0.6 percent of American oil imports—not a very impressive amount and one that could easily be made up elsewhere.

Furthermore, American participation in a "no-fly zone" did not involve a serious military commitment. In fact, it was a tactic chosen more because it was relatively undemanding than because it was effective. And besides, it was endorsed by the Arab League and the United Nations.

What is "R2P"?

In 2005, the UN Security Council adopted a resolution establishing as an international norm a doctrine known as R2P (sometimes rendered RtoP)—responsibility to protect. In the wake of the multiple failures of humanitarian intervention in the 1990s (Bosnia, Somalia, Rwanda), the international community formally recognized the principle that individual governments could not be allowed to abdicate the responsibility to protect their populations from the effects of natural disasters or atrocities, nor could they be permitted to commit those atrocities themselves. Furthermore, it agreed that ultimate responsibility to protect civilians rested with the international community, which has a number of options at its disposal to enforce compliance. These options run the gamut from sanctions and arms embargoes to military intervention. Security Council Resolution 1973, which authorized the air campaign against Qaddafi's forces, explicitly invoked the doctrine, citing "the responsibility of the Libyan authorities to protect the Libyan population."

Although the uprising in Libya amounted to the highest-profile test of R2P so far, it might also have provided the death knell for practical application of the doctrine. The Security Council passed Resolution 1973 to prevent, according to its backers, the impending massacre of innocents in Libya. Critics argue that the decision to take military action was made with undue speed, that the initial proposal to constitute a "no-fly zone" somehow expanded into a more open-ended military commitment, and that

NATO intervention soon went beyond protecting civilians. It became, they argue, regime change hidden behind a humanitarian façade.

Why did efforts to fill the post-uprisings political void in Yemen and Libya flounder?

The "retirement" of Ali Abdullah Saleh and the death of Muammar Qaddafi provided Yemenis and Libyans the opportunity to move on, repair the damage inflicted by civil wars, and reach a consensus about the future of their countries. Instead, attempts to reach agreement on even fundamental issues, such as constitutions, stalled in both countries.

Although outside powers had determined the course of the uprisings in both cases, the manner by which they did so differed. They brokered a truce and national dialogue in Yemen. In contrast, after providing crucial military support that enabled rebels in Libya to obliterate that nation's political leadership (such as it was), they withdrew, leaving an untested transitional government in place. Post-uprising attempts at state-building thus reflected the divergent effects of foreign intervention in the two states: In Yemen, where former regime insiders and the loyal opposition had hijacked the uprising from the Taghrayr protesters early on, the international community acted as if it were more interested in stability than change—which it was. It thus left the pre-uprising power elite intact. In Libya the international community left a political vacuum.

Yemen's National Dialogue Conference was the centerpiece of international efforts at reconstructing Yemen's political system. Although intended to bring together all the stakeholders in Yemeni political life—from established politicians to the youths who had taken to the streets to women and civil society groups—the conference was in fact dominated by the usual suspects. The largest blocs of seats went to the former ruling party and the loyal opposition parties of the JMP. Important players, including Tawakol Karman, a female youth activist whose role in the uprising earned her a Nobel Peace Prize, and prominent members of the southern secession movement, whose cause was perhaps the most important issue on the agenda, absented themselves.

Although the delegates did come up with 1,400 recommendations to be taken up by a constitutional committee appointed by the president, they punted on key issues, such as the southern question. Not that it much mattered: Most Yemenis realized that whatever happened at the conference, real politics would continue to take place outside its chambers. Saleh was still on the scene as leader of the former ruling party. So were Hadi and the Ahmars who, along with the Islah Party, joined forces to make sure Saleh would not make a comeback that would cut into their share of the spoils. None of them had an interest in a real democratic transition, which would have put their ability to milk their cash cow and political power at risk.

The Libyan transition, which began while NATO was raining down its firepower on Qaddafi's forces, started off with great promise. Rebels set up a Libyan Transitional National Council during the combat phase of the uprising. The council reflected the composition of the rebel movement: the heads of local councils established in liberated towns, Islamists and secular academics and lawyers (including Fathi Terbil), reformists and revolutionaries, all united in their opposition to Qaddafi—but, unfortunately, in little else. Elections for a permanent General National Council (GNC) were held in July 2012 to great enthusiasm and a huge turnout. But the GNC and the Libyan government that came from its ranks proved incapable of breaking the power of the various militias that refused to leave the scene and which, in some cases, were the armed wings of parties represented in parliament.

The GNC fell to wrangling over procedural issues, with (shades of Tunisia and Egypt) non-Islamist and Islamist members convinced that their counterparts were conspiring to hijack the revolution. During the summer of 2013, Libyans grew so sickened by the political wrangling and so emboldened by events in Egypt that they stormed the headquarters of both the dominant Islamist and non-Islamist parties, burning the former to the ground and ransacking the latter. With the prime minister declaring a state of emergency, there was no doubt that the scene of real politics was the streets.

Immediately after the fall of Tripoli, militias affiliated with outlying towns roamed the streets of the capital, while Islamist militias—including the Ansar al-Sharia of Libya, which was responsible for the attack on the American consulate and the killing of the American ambassador in September 2012—did the same in Benghazi, reducing Libya's two largest cities to the wild west. Militias in Tripoli even kidnapped the prime minister and deputy intelligence chief in autumn 2013, holding them for a few hours before releasing them, perhaps as a reminder of who really ran things. On the upside, popular protest temporarily drove the militias from Tripoli and the Islamist militias of Benghazi underground. On the downside, without the protection rackets run by the largest of those militias, lawlessness simply spread.

In the end, Yemen and Libya came to share the same three problems that imperiled not only their post-Saleh, post-Qaddafi transitions, but their very existence as states. First, the security situation became dire as both states experienced a wave of politically motivated kidnappings, assassinations, and attacks on vital infrastructure and as jihadi groups established themselves as permanent fixtures in rural areas of Yemen and urban areas of Libya. In Yemen, the violence increasingly took on a sectarian tinge as a variety of religiously identified communities sought to assert or defend themselves or exact revenge in the midst of a total breakdown of government control.

The ongoing violence, along with other factors, exacerbated economic problems in both countries as well. In 2013, the World Economic Forum, citing corruption, violence, political instability, and damage to infrastructure, ranked Yemen's economy as the fourth worst in the world. Strikes, attacks on infrastructure, and the seizure of ports and pipelines by militias disrupted Libya's oil-dependent economy. When a North Korean-flagged tanker set sail from a Libyan port with $30 million worth of oil to be sold on behalf of the militia that controlled that port, US Navy SEALs intercepted it and turned it back. By the end of 2013, Libya had managed to export only roughly one-fifth the amount of oil it had exported before the 2011 revolution (exports picked up in the second half of 2014, however, in spite of the political chaos).

Finally, both Yemen and Libya faced break-up or anarchy, as rival militias battled it out and insurgent groups, watching central power growing even weaker than it had been, challenged governments that refused to abdicate power or respond to the long-standing grievances of those they claimed to represent.

What are the fissures that might divide Yemen in the future?

Citizens feel loyal to a state in part because they participate in common activities and subscribe to a common national myth. States promote common activities and common national myths through state institutions. It therefore stands to reason that a state with weak institutions would be more prone to division than one with strong institutions. This is not to say that the uprisings in Yemen and Libya, which have destroyed the delicate political balance established by Saleh and Qaddafi, will lead to the division of either country. Rather, it is to say that in the wake of the uprisings such a division is possible, particularly as crises drag on and central authority remains absent or weak.

There are two major fault lines in Yemen. First, there is one in the north. At the time of the outbreak of the uprising, the Saleh regime was fighting Houthi rebels there (the rebels took their name from that of a leading Zaydi cleric and his family). The rebels had multiple complaints against the government, including underdevelopment of the north, heavy-handedness on the part of the Saleh regime there, and marginalization of Zaydis at the hands of the government and government-sponsored salafis. Over the course of 2013 and 2014, the Houthis carved out a state within a state for themselves. When the Yemeni government sent its army north, the rebels defeated it and then took the battle to Sana itself, where they occupied key government installations. They forced the government to resign, then extracted a promise from President Hadi that there would be Houthi representation in a new government (the rebels also demanded that the government restore subsidies on fuel, in part to demonstrate that they were fighting for the rights of all Yemenis). Hadi agreed to their demands, but no Yemen-watcher believed this would be the end of the story.

The second fault line—one that threatens the territorial integrity of Yemen—is the one that separates what had been North Yemen from South Yemen. Many residents of the south believe that the unification of the two Yemens had been mishandled. The south did not achieve the representation in government promised it in 1990, and after the 1994 civil war southerners complained that carpetbaggers from the north "colonized" the south, taking positions of power and control over southern resources. And since the largest of Yemen's oil fields lies in the south, their complaints had wide resonance. Government intransigence transformed a protest movement into a movement promoting southern secession, and although the bulk of the southern secession movement has chosen civil disobedience as its main tactic, armed groups have emerged which threaten to reopen the civil war.

Is civil war in Libya in the cards?

A number of factors have contributed to anarchy in Libya. Regional and local loyalties—manifested by the 1,700 locally based militias roaming the country—often trump national loyalty; the Berber community, which makes up about 10 percent of the population and was repressed under Qaddafi, has been restive; and the faultline dividing Tripolitania from Cyrenaica—Tripoli from Benghazi—which hardened under Qaddafi remains. To this day, westerners boast of their (relative) cosmopolitanism and complain of the tribalism and Islamism of the east, while easterners take pride in the fact that the uprising broke out on their turf and *they* liberated Tripoli.

Just as serious, as in Egypt a coalition that included disparate groupings united solely by their desire to get rid of an autocrat fragmented into Islamist and anti-Islamist camps. As in Egypt, "regime remnants" joined the anti-Islamist camp. The Islamists came to dominate the GNC through a "political isolation law," which prohibited anyone associated with the Qaddafi government from participating in politics (Qaddafi hardly invited Islamists into his inner circle, so this was a boon to their ambitions). They managed to do this mostly through threats and physical intimidation, which led the anti-Islamist camp to harden its position against them.

In May 2014, the main non-Islamist militia, the Libyan National Army (LNA), stormed parliament, while the parliamentarians called on pro-Islamist Libyan Shield brigades for protection. Both sides had their foreign enablers: for the LNA, it was Egypt, the UAE, and Saudi Arabia, which lumped all Islamist groups, from the Muslim Brotherhood to Ansar al-Sharia, in the same terrorist category; for the Libyan Shield brigades it was Qatar, which never met an Islamist group it didn't like. A month later, Libyans elected a parliament in which Islamists won only thirty seats out of two hundred. Undeterred, Islamist militias seized control of Tripoli, forced the parliament to flee to Tobruk in eastern

Libya, and set up a government of their own. With two governments claiming to represent the legitimate aspirations of the Libyan people, the country hovered on the brink of civil war.

Why is al-Qaeda in Yemen?

Estimates of the number of al-Qaeda members in Yemen range from several hundred fighters to several thousand. Some are Yemeni, others come from Saudi Arabia or further afield. Yemen is the ancestral home of the bin Laden family, but this, of course, does not explain the current presence of al-Qaedists there. They are there for other reasons. First, the pressure put on al-Qaeda in Saudi Arabia after 9/11 forced al-Qaedists out of the kingdom and over the border into Yemen. In 2009, they joined forces with Yemeni al-Qaedists to found a local franchise known as "al-Qaeda in the Arabian Peninsula." The organization gained a territorial foothold in Yemen's badlands soon thereafter, in part by playing the game of tribal politics, in part by bribing local tribal leaders who were not averse to selling their loyalties to the highest bidder.

In addition, the government itself had prepared the ground for al-Qaeda by encouraging the spread of salafism. Ali Abdullah Saleh supported the spread of salafi schools and organizations to check the power of his opponents, particularly the political Left and Yemen's Zaydi population. That is, until they too represented a threat. By then, however, it was too late. While it is the rare salafi or even Islamist who agrees with al-Qaeda's idiosyncratic message (the real enemy is the far enemy, the Crusader-Zionist conspiracy; nation states must be abolished, etc.), and while it might even be argued that al-Qaeda represents a fringe of a fringe of salafis, the spread of salafism and the empowerment of salafis created a supportive environment for al-Qaeda.

The final reason al-Qaeda has established a presence in Yemen is strategic. Although al-Qaeda distinguishes itself from other Islamist organizations by a lack of interest in taking over states per se, it does seek to implant itself in territories over which governments have little or no control so as to harass and thus exhaust the Crusader-Zionist conspiracy and its agents. Yemen, with a weak central government and rough terrain, thus provides an ideal location for the group (as do the outreaches of Libya).

Just how powerful al-Qaeda is in Yemen is debatable, though. On occasion there are reports that al-Qaeda-type groups, if not al-Qaeda in the Arabian Peninsula itself, have taken over towns in the south as a first step toward establishing an "Islamic emirate" there; that is, a base from which al-Qaeda could continue its battle against the Crusader-Zionist conspiracy. These reports may or may not be accurate: events in the south reflect the al-Qaeda *modus operandi*, but no one knows for sure who is actually behind them. In the past, the Yemeni government has exaggerated al-Qaeda presence and activities to representatives of the United States, from which it has received generous support for its antiterrorism efforts. It is thus possible that the government blamed al-Qaeda for acts committed by others, including unaffiliated militants, tribes, and even government agents.

Is al-Qaeda in Libya?

There is an al-Qaeda presence in western Libya, by the Algerian border, where an official al-Qaeda franchise, al-Qaeda in the Islamic Maghreb (*maghreb* is Arabic for North Africa) has established encampments. Again, any non-policed space will do for al-Qaeda. In 2012, the organization worked with local groups in Mali, which fought to establish an independent state in the north of that country. Benefiting from weapons looted from Qaddafi's arsenals, that alliance almost succeeded in partitioning the country—until French and African Union armies intervened on the side of the central government.

Then there is the vexing question of the relationship between Ansar al-Sharia in Libya and al-Qaeda. Since September 11, and particularly since the death of bin Laden, al-Qaeda has become more decentralized. In addition, groups claiming to be al-Qaeda have popped up throughout the region, whether or not they receive al-Qaeda's blessing, and still other groups have emulated al-Qaeda's tactics. While a number of Obama's domestic opponents fume that al-Qaeda in the guise of Ansar al-Sharia was responsible for the attack on the American consulate in Benghazi in 2012, Ansar al-Sharia does not claim affiliation with al-Qaeda, has not been recognized by al-Qaeda central as an affiliate, and has serious ideological disagreements with al-Qaeda on a host of issues, including al-Qaeda's refusal to work within the context of a nation-state.

It very well may be that al-Qaeda, which had never drawn up a sophisticated organizational chart, is changing, or that al-Qaeda central no longer has the heft it once had, or that ideology—the only real glue that held al-Qaeda together—is no longer important, or that the dispute about whether Ansar al-Sharia is al-Qaeda is distinction without difference. Or it might be that we should take Ansar al-Sharia at its word.

How did Libya affect American and Russian policy in Syria?

Both the United States and Russia learned lessons from the Libyan rebellion which they applied to the Syria crisis—with devastating results.

The Americans called what happened in Libya—the lack of preparation in Libya for the day after, the breakdown of law and order and continued violence, and the absence of authoritative government institutions that could deal with problems from security to the economy—a "hard landing," something they wished to avoid at all costs in Syria. Since there was little support in the United States for putting boots on the ground to separate the combatants or ensure a smooth transition in Syria, the United States embraced the idea of bringing together members of the "moderate" opposition with the "less bad" members of the Syrian government to negotiate a settlement that would bring about the formation of a transitional government. A ceasefire and the maintenance of essential services and institutions—from security to banking—would result in a "soft landing" for Syria, enabling that country to avoid the fate of Libya.

Unfortunately, that policy is doomed to failure for multiple reasons—as the debacle of the Geneva II talks attended by representatives of the Syrian government and some of the opposition in the summer of 2013 demonstrated. But spooked by the shadow of Libya, the United States stubbornly stuck to its guns.

The Russians, too, learned a lesson from Libya. Counting on NATO to observe the terms of UN Resolution 1973 that established a no-fly zone over Libya, the Russians (and the Chinese) abstained in the Security Council, allowing the resolution to pass. But the no-fly zone was unworkable. Qaddafi did not have to use his air force against the rebels—he was inflicting enough damage with helicopters, tanks, and artillery. So NATO abandoned the no-fly zone strategy and instead began close combat assistance to the rebels—something the Russians never signed on for. In answer to the question, "Why have the Russians blocked every significant UN resolution on Syria?" the answer is: They felt they had been badly burned on Libya.

4

"COUP-PROOFED"

BAHRAIN AND SYRIA

What do Bahrain and Syria have in common?

Like Tunisia and Egypt, Bahrain and Syria make an unlikely pair. Bahrain is an archipelago of thirty-two islands in the Persian Gulf. The largest—Bahrain—is roughly three and a half times the size of Washington, DC. It would take 282 Bahrains to fill the land mass occupied by Syria. The number of citizens of Bahrain (inhabitants minus guest workers) is 2.5 percent of the number of Syrians. And whereas Bahrain is a kingdom, since its inception Syria has been a republic.

Bahrain's economy has historically been heavily dependent on oil exports, which make up more than 70 percent of government revenues. Seeing the handwriting on the wall in terms of diminishing reserves and diminishing demand, Bahrain began diversifying in recent years, encouraging the growth of a dynamic financial sector. A modest oil producer at best, Syria was heavily invested in agriculture before the outbreak of the uprising. And even before the uprising no one in their right mind would have considered Syria a safe haven for their money. After all, in 2010 Syria tied with Belarus and Uganda, among others, for 127th place on the index of financial transparency compiled by Transparency International.[1]

In terms of external alliances, Bahrain is closely allied with the other Gulf states, particularly nearby Saudi Arabia, as well as the United States. As a matter of fact, Bahrain is the home port of the US Navy's Fifth Fleet, providing an undisclosed, but substantial, revenue stream to the island nation for leasing rights. Syria, on the other hand, proudly boasts its membership in the anti-imperialist "resistance camp" in the region, alongside Iran and Hizbullah, the militant Lebanese Shi'i political association-cum-party-cum-militia. It is still technically at war with Israel and has close relations with Russia, which has its only Mediterranean-based naval facility at the Syrian port city of Tartus.

Historically, too, Bahrain and Syria have had different trajectories. During the eighteenth century, members of the Khalifa family, along with other families and tribes caught up in that century's great tribal migrations, conquered the island of Bahrain, ending two centuries of Persian rule. The conquest severed Bahrain from Persia, but it connected the island with the conquest's launch site, the peninsula that would become Qatar. During the nineteenth century, the inhabitants of the mainland rebelled, and even though the Bahrainis put down the rebellion the British, concerned as always with maintaining stability on the route to India, used the Bahraini reinvasion of the peninsula as a justification to intervene (this was the origin of a separate state of Qatar). The British established both Bahrain and Qatar as protectorates, a status they held until 1971, when they became independent.

In 1971 Britain implemented its "East of Suez" policy, so named because the British, responding to economic pressures, withdrew from their bases in the Middle East and Asia— that is, their bases east of Suez. Upon the British withdrawal, Bahrain, Qatar, and the principalities that would form the United Arab Emirates (UAE) attempted to unify. When those attempts failed, each became an independent state, and the Khalifas continued their role as dynastic rulers of Bahrain, which they remain to this day.

Under the Ottoman Empire, "Greater Syria" was a geographic notion, not a political unit. Greater Syria consisted of the territories that would become Syria, Lebanon, Israel, Palestine, and Jordan. With the dismantling of the Ottoman Empire in the wake of World War I, Britain and France divided up its territories and held on to them as League of Nations mandates—sort of temporary colonies purportedly created so that "advanced nations" might prepare their charges to face "the strenuous conditions of the modern world." Britain took administrative control of the territory that would become Jordan, Israel, and Palestine; France took the territory which they would divide into Lebanon and Syria. Syria received its independence in 1946.

Unlike Bahrain, which has been under the control of the Khalifa dynasty since the eighteenth century, post-independence Syria was the most unstable state in the Arab world, undergoing ten coups d'état between independence and 1970. That was when Hafez al-Assad, the father of the current president of Syria, Bashar al-Assad, took power and stabilized the country. Part of the reason for Syria's instability was its novelty as a state—there had never been a sovereign entity called Syria before 1946, and Syria's current borders were finalized for the most part (the exception being the territory lost to Israel in 1967) only in 1937. Another reason was the ambitions of regional players, initially Jordan, then Egypt, which briefly united with Syria in the United Arab Republic (1958–61). And cold war competition between the United States and the Soviet Union did not help either. As discussed earlier, the United States in effect sponsored the first postwar coup d'état in the Arab world when it backed an ambitious colonel who seized power in 1949.

In spite of all these differences, however, there are two factors Bahrain and Syria hold in common that ensured the uprisings there would initially follow similar trajectories: the heterogeneity of the two countries and their rule by members of religious minorities, on the one hand, and the strategies their rulers used to stay in power, on the other.

About 70 percent of the Bahraini population is Shi'i Muslim. Most of the remainder is Sunni. In Syria, about 75 percent of the population is Sunni. The remainder is divided among Alawites (followers of an offshoot of Shi'i Islam), who make up about 13 percent of the population, Christians, who make up about 10–12 percent of the population, and others. And in both places minorities—Sunnis in Bahrain, Alawites in Syria—control the reins of government while majorities complain of discrimination, higher unemployment, lack of government services, and other injustices.

Despite popular belief, sectarian hostility or even conflict is not a universal default position among Arabs. Nevertheless, rule by minorities does affect the strategies adopted by rulers as well as political choices made by members of minority communities.

Rulers can claim legitimacy by blackmail, soliciting the support of minorities by fueling fears that their rights or even their lives could be jeopardized should the majority come to power. Thus, they could count on minority communities—not just the ones from which they hail but all minority communities—to circle their wagons in support of the minority-controlled regime. During the uprisings, both the Bahraini and Syrian governments have relied heavily on the support provided by minority communities. The Syrian government has gone so far as to arm "popular committees" made up of inhabitants of Alawite villages to act as a self-defense force and relieve the Syrian army of the burden of defending those villages itself. It has also enjoyed the support of many Christians.

What is "coup-proofing"?

The second characteristic both states hold in common and which affected the course of the uprisings there was the manner by which autocrats made their regimes nearly impregnable from assault from within.

Hafez al-Assad remade the most unstable Arab state into one of the most stable. He then passed off control of that state to his son whose regime has survived pretty much intact even when confronted with widespread rebellion. The Khalifa family has maintained control over Bahrain in spite of the rebelliousness of its population. Why didn't one part of the Bahraini and Syrian regimes turn on another, as had happened in Tunisia and Egypt, or simply fragment, as in Yemen and Libya?

The answer is that the Khalifa dynasty and Hafez al-Assad "coup-proofed" their regimes.[2] Coup-proofing involves a series of steps a leader might take in order to protect himself. In Bahrain and Syria (and in Saddam Hussein's Iraq and elsewhere), it centered on two processes: distribution of "coup-critical positions" to trusted members of family and religious sect, and the creation of armed forces parallel to the regular military along with multiple security agencies having overlapping jurisdiction.

Although there are two main branches to the ruling family in Bahrain, regime survival is critical to both and members of that family occupy the most important positions of governance. Looking at the online "Chiefs of State and Cabinet Members of Foreign Governments" published by the CIA, one is struck by how many members of the Bahraini government have the same last name, "al-Khalifa"[3]: king; prime minister; first deputy prime minister; three deputy prime ministers; ministers of culture, finance, foreign affairs, interior, justice and Islamic affairs, royal court, royal court for follow-up affairs (!), royal court affairs, and defense affairs. Then there are those in the security and military establishment: the supreme commander, commander in chief, and chief of staff of the armed forces are also family members, as are the head of the Bahrain Police Directorate and the minister in charge of the Public Security Forces.

The situation is similar in Syria, where members of Assad's extended family and sect make up the core of the inner governing circle and are distributed in high places throughout the government and military. Bashar's cousin, Dhu al-Himma Shalish, is the head of the presidential guard, while his brother, Maher, is commander of the Republican Guard and Fourth Armored Division and Assef Shawkat, his brother-in-law, was deputy chief of staff before his death in a bombing. None of them could have turned on the regime; if the regime goes, they would go too. As a matter of fact, few persons of note have defected from the regime and, of those who have—one brigadier general, a prime minister (which in Syria is a post of little importance) and an ambassador to Iraq—not one was Alawite.

Both the Syrian and Bahraini regimes have created multiple military units with separate chains of command—such as Shalish's presidential guard and Maher al-Assad's Republican Guard—on which, when push came to shove, the regime could count. Military and state security responsibilities in Bahrain are similarly dispersed, with some units of the military/security apparatus under the control of one of the two major family factions while others have been delegated to the other. In this way the Khalifas have achieved a balance, and whatever intramural disagreements there might be between the so-called "reform" and "security" branches of the family, both realize the price of disloyalty. The various units they command also follow different chains of command, some reaching up to the Ministry of Defense, others to the Ministry of the Interior, still others to the National Security Agency.

Because the local Sunni community is small, and because the Bahraini government believes most Shi'is are not to be trusted with military or security responsibilities, key units of the defense and security apparatus consist of Sunnis imported from outside the country. Some of them receive citizenship in return for their service. This has been called "political naturalization." It is limited to foreign Sunnis who serve the government and is one of the issues that has bred resentment among Bahraini Shi'is who believe that the regime is attempting to shift the demographic balance between Sunnis and Shi'is. Thus, the Special Security Force Command consists of Arabs from Jordan, Syria, and elsewhere, who serve alongside Pakistanis, and the National Guard is predominantly Pakistani. Outsiders who know on which side their bread is buttered tend to be trustworthy, and the National Guard played a critical role in putting down the initial phase of the uprising.

In addition, both regimes have relied on informal security forces that hail from minority communities to do their dirty work. In Bahrain, there are the baltagiya, who perform the same duties their counterparts in Egypt had. In Syria, there are the dreaded *shabiha* (a word related to the Arabic word for "ghosts"), black-clad security goons who come from Assad's hometown and its immediate vicinity. They too are fiercely loyal. Like members of the inner circle, they cannot turn on the regime, because if the regime goes, so will they.

Coup-proofing in Bahrain and Syria is important for understanding the uprisings because it narrowed the possible outcomes of the uprisings in each state to one of three possibilities: the complete destruction of the regime, the complete destruction of the opposition, or stalemate.

Why did Bahrain's February protests end so tragically?

In the wake of events in Tunisia and Egypt, Bahraini activists, taking advantage of the anonymity of social media, called for their own Day of Rage protests to be held in the capital, Manama, and elsewhere on February 14. Protesters demanded constitutional reform, free elections, release of prisoners of conscience, and an end to torture (a Human Rights Watch report from 2010 had warned of "a return to full blown authoritarianism" in Bahrain).[4] They also made two other demands that the regime seized on to characterize the movement as sectarian: they demanded a truly representative consultative council (which, if truly representative, would have meant a majority Shi'i council), and an end to political naturalization.

The regime claimed these demands proved that Iran and its Bahraini agents were behind the protests.

The charge was unfounded and subsequent events added a touch of irony to the allegation that foreign interference was at the root of Bahrain's problems. In the end, it was the predominantly non-Bahraini and non-Bahraini-born security forces that broke up the February 14 protests throughout the country, drawing the first blood in a village in the north, then again at the victim's funeral procession the next day.

In Manama, organizers attempted to make the Pearl Square roundabout their Tahrir Square (pearl diving was Bahrain's most important industry before the invention of artificial pearls in the early twentieth century and the discovery of oil, and a huge monument with a pearl on top marked the roundabout). The security forces dispersed the protesters the first day, but when news of the killings spread the crowds grew. As members of legal and illegal political associations and Bahrainis from nearby villages descended on the roundabout, Pearl Square came to resemble as much a street fair as the site of a political protest, just as Tahrir Square had in the waning days of the Egyptian protests. And as in the case of their Egyptian counterparts, Bahrainis occupying the square stuck as much as possible to a tactic of nonviolence, even in the face of provocation by baltagiya.

Nevertheless, the government also learned a lesson from the Egyptian protests: clear the square. In the early morning of the fourth day, security forces stormed the roundabout, killing four, some reportedly as they slept.

The storming of Pearl Square was the first of two events that transformed the nature of the Bahraini uprising. Its effects were seen in a number of ways. Over the course of the next month, the number of protesters in downtown Manama swelled as associations of engineers, lawyers, and teachers, along with politicians and trade unionists, joined the protests. More significantly, the momentum of the protests shifted from those willing to engage in a dialogue with the regime (such as the largest of the legal political associations) to those calling for the downfall of the regime (such as the largest of the illegal political associations and many of the original protest organizers). In addition, although the slogans chanted by the protesters remained intersectarian, Shi'i religious leaders and grassroots organizers increasingly took the public stage.

The second event that transformed the nature of the uprising came in the wake of a planned march from the square to Manama's financial district. After the storming of the square, the confrontation between the government and the protesters had settled into a stalemate, with hardliners inside and outside the government pressing to finish the job and others inside and outside the government pressing for compromise. The Bahraini prime minister and government of Saudi Arabia were in the first grouping, the Bahraini king and the government of the United States in the latter. The former grouping took the day.

Exactly one month after the protests began, a thousand troops from Saudi Arabia and five hundred policemen from the UAE crossed the causeway linking Bahrain with the mainland and took up positions around government buildings, freeing up Bahrain's own military and security forces to partake in a binge of repression. The Saudi and Emirati forces that entered Bahrain did so under the umbrella of a joint military force known as Peninsula Shield, which the GCC had established to deter and respond to aggression against any member state—in this case, Iranian aggression against Bahrain.

A commission of inquiry appointed by the king would later find no evidence for this claim.

What occurred in Bahrain in the wake of the crackdown?

After the entry of Saudi and Emirati forces into Bahrain, the regime engaged in a two-pronged effort to silence the opposition. First, it staged a series of "national dialogues" that have, to date, come to naught. In its first incarnation, the regime invited an unwieldy three hundred delegates, of which only about thirty-five represented the formal opposition (no one who initiated the Pearl Square protests participated); in its third, the regime attempted to stack the deck by inviting an equal number of delegates from a pro-regime parliamentary bloc, a pro-regime "nationalist" bloc, and an opposition bloc. The king refused to attend, the role of the government in the process has been unclear, and the fate of any recommendations uncertain. What is certain is that no national dialogue will produce significant change so long as the regime holds the upper hand in the streets.

The regime has also expanded its repertoire of repression. Regime opponents face mass arrests and long prison sentences; all demonstrations have been declared illegal; insulting the king can result in a prison sentence of up to seven years; the security forces have cordoned off recalcitrant villages; punishments for crimes against the state have been expanded to include the revocation of citizenship; and the government keeps the media, NGOs, and charitable organizations on a short leash. On top of it all, the regime has declared war on social media, arresting cyberactivists, blocking or shutting down internet access, and even setting up a hotline so that citizens might report websites and social media accounts that "act against the public interest."

Sometimes measures taken by the regime border on the comic: it is illegal to possess a Guy Fawkes mask (used globally to disguise anarchists and members of occupy movements), for example, and in October 2013 the regime attempted to purchase 1.6 million tear gas canisters. The Bahraini population in its entirety is 1.3 million.

Regime repression has had three effects on oppositional activity in Bahrain. First, since the regime has identified the "enemy" as Iran and Iran's fifth column in Bahrain (the Shi'i community), the focal point of rebellion and counterinsurgency became that community and the political groups it spawned. In other words, what had begun as an intersectarian struggle against autocracy became sectarianized as Shi'is responded to government targeting and repression in kind. Second, the protests became more violent as car-bombings became commonplace and sporadic demonstrations held in urban areas descended into street battles. Finally, the main sites of protest have moved out of the cities, which are heavily guarded and periodically under lockdown, to numerous Shi'i villages, where anti-regime activity might be contained but cannot be eradicated.

How did the uprising in Syria begin?

The beginning of the uprising in Syria bears a closer resemblance to the beginning of the uprising in Libya than to that in Egypt. Whereas protesters in Egypt made the capital city, Cairo, the symbolic center of the uprising, in Syria, as in Libya, the uprising broke out in the provinces. This was not simply because regimes in the latter two countries concentrated the repressive apparatus in their capitals. After all, such was the case in Egypt as well. More to the point, unlike the uprising in Egypt, the uprising in Syria, like the one in Libya, did not take place in the wake of meticulous preparation. It was spontaneous.

This is not to say there were not attempts to plan an Egypt-style protest in Syria. Beginning in January 2011, social-networking youths, similar to those who participated in the Egyptian protests, organized anemic demonstrations which failed to capture the public's imagination. A group calling itself "Syrian Revolution 2011 against Bashar al-Assad" organized one such demonstration in Damascus on March 15. Protesters demanded, among other things, that the government rescind the emergency law and release political prisoners. It attracted only an estimated 200 to 350 protesters and was easily broken up by security forces. Then, four days later, all hell broke loose.

In the first week of March, security forces had arrested ten schoolchildren aged fifteen or younger in the dusty provincial city of Daraa. Their crime? Borrowing a slogan from the Egyptian revolution, they had written, "Down with the regime (nizam)" on a wall. They were imprisoned and, while in prison, tortured. For about two weeks their families attempted to gain their release. Then they took to the streets. Security forces opened fire, killing several. The next day, their funeral procession brought out twenty thousand demonstrators—in a city of seventy-seven thousand—who chanted antigovernment slogans and attacked government buildings.

The government understood the seriousness of the protests immediately and sent out a delegation to meet with community members. The delegation heard their grievances, which by that time had expanded from the abducted children and the murder of their parents to economic and political demands. It promised to act on them. Unfortunately for the government, soon after the meeting security forces murdered fifteen worshippers at a local mosque, thus undercutting the delegation's attempt to defuse the crisis.

Coincidentally, protests erupted in the northern coastal city of Banias on the same day the anguished parents went out on the streets in Daraa. As in the case of the Daraa protests, the protests in Banias initially reflected local concerns (the secular regime had cracked down on female schoolteachers there who wore the *niqab*, the Syrian variant of the veil), then, like their compatriots in Daraa, protesters expanded their focus to national issues, such as the brutality of the regime, the absence of democratic institutions, and corruption.

Protests soon spread to the coastal city of Latakia, then to Duma, north of the capital, where protesters aired similar grievances and met with the same violence. In village after village, town after town, protesters took to the streets as word spread of their neighbors' boldness and the regime's response. Eventually, protests reached the suburbs of Damascus and Syria's largest city, Aleppo.

Who is Bashar al-Assad?

As hard as it is to believe now, before the uprising Bashar al-Assad enjoyed a reputation as a reformer. His father, Hafez al-Assad, who governed Syria from 1970 until his death in 2000, groomed Bashar's much-despised elder brother to succeed him. When the brother died in an automobile accident, Hafez recalled Bashar from London, where he had been studying ophthalmology, and gave him a crash course on politics. After the elder Assad died, parliament amended the constitution, reducing the minimum age for president from forty to thirty-four—which was, not coincidentally, Bashar's exact age. Soon after acceding to power, Bashar oversaw the brief "Damascus Spring," a period of time when the government took a rather benign view of unsupervised political organizing and free expression. And when the Damascus Spring turned into the Damascus Winter, it was Hafez al-Assad's old cronies who took most of the blame.

How did the Syrian regime deal with the uprising?

Like other regimes, the Syrian regime has taken a carrot-and-stick approach to the uprising. However, the carrots offered have been too little, too late, and met with widespread skepticism anyway. And as the rebellion descended into full-fledged civil war, the regime offered fewer carrots and wielded ever-larger sticks.

The reforms the regime offered the protesters were piecemeal and cosmetic. For example, the government offered up a new constitution in 2012 that ended the monopoly on power held by the Baath Party, of which Hafez al-Assad had been a member. Unfortunately, the constitution maintains the president's right to appoint all functionaries of the government, confirms his role as high commander of the armed forces and head of the judiciary, and grants him the right to dissolve parliament should he choose.

The government also repealed the hated emergency law that had been in effect since the Baath ascendancy in 1963. The law allowed the government to override the constitution and criminal code and to suspend habeas corpus (that is, to detain those accused of crimes indefinitely). It was thus used as the legal basis to clamp down on the protests, and its repeal had been one of the principal demands of the early uprising. Although the government rescinded the law, however, it did not rescind presidential decrees that were equally onerous. One such decree put members of the security forces beyond prosecution; another made membership in the Syrian Muslim Brotherhood a crime punishable by death. In the end, annulment of the emergency law did little to curb the government's bloodlust.

The offer of these carrots undercut the regime's own explanation for the uprising. The government blamed the troubles on salafis, al-Qaedists, ex-convicts, smugglers, armed gangs, and an international conspiracy involving everyone from the United States to Israel to Saudi Arabia. (There are credible reports that the regime freed imprisoned al-Qaeda-types so they might wreak havoc and discredit the opposition.) Why offer carrots if these elements, and not regime policies, were responsible for the uprising? Blaming the uprising on Islamists, criminals, and foreigners also turned protesters into outlaws and justified for the regime and its loyalists the stomach-churning brutality that the government applied to quell it. Here is how CNN reported one such act of brutality, the murder of thirteen-year-old Hamza al-Khatib:

On April 29, demonstrators from villages surrounding Daraa, Syria, marched on the city in an attempt to break the Syrian military siege there. . . . On that day, eyewitnesses say, security forces fired indiscriminately on them, killing and wounding dozens. Countless others were detained in a mass roundup. Among them, says his family, was Hamza. He got separated from his father in the chaos. A month later, the family received his body. The video was taken at that time by a relative, the family says. Much of the video of the child's corpse is too graphic to broadcast. His face is bloated and purple. His body is covered in bruises. There are gunshot wounds to his torso, and his genitals are mutilated.[5]

The regime intended the murder of al-Khatib to serve as a warning to those who dared defy it. It had the opposite effect: about two weeks after the government turned over the child's body, protesters elsewhere took to the streets shouting a slogan reminiscent of the Egyptian uprising: "We are all Hamza al-Khatib!"

How did the regime sectarianize the uprising?

At the start of the uprising the government relied on the formal security services, along with the *shabiha*, to quell the disturbances. It also organized armed "popular committees" to protect Alawite villages, and equipped pro-regime vigilantes with knives and clubs to be used in street battles with mostly unarmed protesters. Relying on formal and informal security groups, along with pro-regime vigilantes, all of which were identified with the Alawite community, had an effect that the government undoubtedly foresaw and cynically exploited: it sectarianized the conflict and secured the unqualified loyalty of much of the Alawite and Christian communities who feared the worst should the regime fall.

Members of the formal and informal security apparatus also provoked tit-for-tat sectarian violence to validate the regime's claim that those fighting it were Islamists, not democrats. In July 2011, nine died in Homs after an Alawite mob surrounded a Sunni mosque in one of the first recorded instances of sectarian conflict during the uprising. That was just a harbinger of worse to come: in Baida and Banias, for example, shabiha massacred 248 Sunnis, and in the village of Aqrab opposition fighters slaughtered at least 125 Alawites.

How did the regime militarize the uprising?

In the beginning, the regime depended most heavily on the security services to put down the uprising. Then, in January 2012 the government shifted tactics. Realizing that its campaign to isolate and punish pockets of resistance using lightly armed security personnel had done little to stamp out the resistance, the regime brought in the heavy artillery—literally. The regime handed counterinsurgency over to the armed forces which, in the manner of militaries throughout the world, are more adept at wielding a meat cleaver than a scalpel.

Scorched-earth tactics were the order of the day, and the test case proved to be the district of Baba Amro in the city of Homs, which called itself the capital of the revolution. Using all the firepower under its command—from tanks, helicopter gunships, and artillery to mortars, heavy machine guns, and snipers—the army first cut off the city from the outside world, then softened up the rebel stronghold, reducing much of it to rubble, and finally stormed it, killing about 250 rebels and driving the remainder out.

Its mission a success, the military began applying the same tactics elsewhere, escalating the level of violence with the occasional use of poison gas and barrel bombs (barrels filled with TNT that are dropped from the air indiscriminately). Partly as a result of these tactics, the government was able to regain the momentum. By 2014 it was in control of the line of cities that stretched from Damascus in the south to Aleppo in the north. The government also dominated the coastal areas to the west, particularly those heavily populated by Alawites. Unable to seize control of much of the countryside and border areas, however, the government proved incapable of uprooting the resistance once and for all.

The military was not the only force that learned a lesson from the change in tactics. As it became increasingly clear that the brutality of the regime against its own citizens knew no bounds, the resistance also changed in form. At the outset, protests had been localized and, in large measure, peaceful affairs. Each rebel village or district had its own "local coordination committee." To protect demonstrations from snipers and informants, protesters staged rallies at night, and organized militias, made up of local fighters who had deserted from the Syrian army, to provide further protection. This proved futile once the army replaced the security services as the regime's main tool to combat the uprising. With their communities under siege or bombardment, local militias were often forced to retreat from their own neighborhoods and regroup and fight wherever they sensed regime vulnerability. The close connection between local militias and their civilian counterparts thus ended, as did any restraint on the part of the military units that grew out of the militias. The civilians lost control of the uprising, and the balance of power within the opposition tipped in favor of the fighters.

Who is the "moderate opposition" in Syria?

Explaining the Syrian opposition is like nailing jello to a wall. It is shape shifting, ideologically heterogeneous, and has evolved (and continues to evolve) as the uprising has evolved. Thus, the local coordination committees, which sprang up in seventy cities throughout Syria to coordinate nonviolent protests at the beginning of the uprising, found themselves sidelined as the conflict became increasingly militarized. So have the protesters who still demonstrate on a regular basis in liberated towns and urban quarters, and other peaceful advocates for human rights and democratic transition, such as Syrian Revolution 2011 and the Syrian Observatory for Human Rights, which bears witness and keeps a running count of the dead and injured. By the third anniversary of the uprising one thousand (!) armed groups made up of upwards of 120,000 combatants dominated the opposition movement.

In addition, both political and military groups are highly fractious, some dissolving under internal or external pressure, others joining in various coalitions which all too often are ephemeral. Thus, the Syrian Islamic Liberation Front (founded September 2012)—a coalition of Islamist militias—morphed into the Syrian Islamic Front (December 2012), which, in turn, morphed into the Islamic Front (September 2013) as conditions changed, groups left or joined or were blackballed, and rival outside powers such as Saudi Arabia and Qatar played their hands.

The National Coalition for Syrian Revolutionary and Opposition Forces (called the Syrian National Coalition for short) is, at least on paper, the supreme coordinating body recognized by most of the international community as the sole, legitimate political representative of a unified opposition. It is the second such organization, the first (the Syrian National Council) distrusted by many inside and outside Syria who suspected it of being a tool of Qatar and the Syrian Muslim Brotherhood. The National Coalition was founded at the encouragement of the "Friends of Syria Group" in order to allow foreign powers to channel assistance to moderate opposition forces efficiently, coordinate the efforts of politicians who mainly reside outside Syria with military commanders on the ground, and enable the opposition to speak with a single voice in international councils. (The Friends of Syria Group consists of more than one hundred nations who needed a venue to plot Syria policy outside the United Nations where Russia has veto power).

Consisting mainly of exiles, the National Coalition has little influence in Syria. On the other hand, a group calling itself the National Coordination Committee for the Forces for Democratic Change (NCC) works entirely within Syria. Made up largely of veteran dissidents and leftists, it initially presented itself as the alternative to the Syrian National

Council. Whereas the latter sought foreign intervention and the overthrow of Assad and his cronies, for example, the NCC opposed intervention and has held a series of dialogues with the regime. It is for this reason that the exile groups have shunned them as collaborators. In the unlikely event of a negotiated settlement, it is probable that the government and the remainder of the opposition would tap members of this group to participate in a transitional government. In the meantime, the militarization of the uprising has sidelined them as well.

If the National Coalition represents the moderate political wing of the opposition, the Supreme Military Council (SMC) serves the same function for the opposition's military wing. In theory, the SMC was formed to coordinate the activities of the Free Syrian Army (FSA). The FSA originally consisted of those deserters from the regular Syrian army who, in the early days of the uprising, banded together on a local level to protect demonstrators from snipers deployed by the regime. Over time, moderate Islamist fighters, drawn to the cities from the hinterlands, joined the FSA as well.

The SMC has had a checkered history and at one point was even temporarily disbanded by the National Coalition which charged it with rampant corruption. Corruption has been only one of its problems. Its existence has been marked by squabbles among its members and defections (the defection of groups that joined the Islamic Front—the largest militias under the SMC—was a particularly devastating blow). Furthermore, the SMC has never been able to assert its authority or coordinate activities among local units which are jealous of their prerogatives. The SMC has proved so inept that in December 2013 the United States suspended aid shipments after Islamist militias raided an SMC warehouse where it stored American-donated supplies. As a result, when the Obama administration announced in September 2014 that it would beef up assistance and training for moderate opposition forces fighting Islamic extremists in Syria, it sidestepped the

SMC and set up a new organization, the Military Operations Command.

What is the Islamist opposition in Syria like?

By far the largest and most effective militias currently on the battlefield are Islamist. Calling militias Islamist, however, is of little value, since this label applies to relatively moderate groupings, such as those that had split from the Free Syrian Army to join the Islamic Front (which also falls under the heading "moderate"), to Jabhat al-Nusra (Support Front), an al-Qaeda affiliate which has nevertheless scrapped important parts of al-Qaeda dogma. It also applies to the "Islamic State" (IS)—formerly the Islamic State of Iraq and Syria (ISIS)—whose harsh application of Islamic law in areas under its control revolted even Jabhat al-Nusra. And as is so commonly the case among the Syrian opposition, it is often the choice of paymaster—Turkey, Qatar, Saudi Arabia, or independent Gulf-based financiers—rather than principled stance that determines the location of an individual or group on the moderate-to-radical spectrum.

Islamist groups also vary in size, from the Islamic Front's 50,000 fighters at the beginning of 2014 to IS's 8,000 to 10,000, a number that increased subsequently as a result of its battlefield victories (by the end of September 2014, the CIA estimate put the number of IS fighters at 31,000, which seems a bit high). The larger and more powerful groups and alliances maintain large swathes of land and villages as fiefdoms from which they extract resources while they fight the regime and, all too often, each other. In this, they are no different from the larger and more powerful non-Islamist militias. Little wonder, then, that some of the most contested territory has been in the oil-producing regions of the country in the east. As one Syrian activist put it, "Two and a half years into the revolt, opposition-held Syria is Mad Max meets The Sopranos."[6]

Moderation is, of course, in the eye of the beholder. The goal of the moderate Islamists is to topple the regime and establish an Islamic state. In its founding statement, the Islamic Front also asserted that the status of men and women are equal, but added the phrase "according to the women's special characteristics in keeping with Islamic law," which certainly muddies the waters. These planks in the Islamic Front's platform also fit well with Jabhat al-Nusra's stated goals, which is odd considering al-Qaeda does not believe that entities like Syria should even exist (in its view the Crusader-Zionist conspiracy imposed states in the Islamic world to keep it divided and weak), and toppling a regime is hardly a worthy objective for an organization that sets its sights higher.

What is the "Islamic State"?

IS—formerly ISIS—is the latest incarnation of the jihadi/*takfiri* movement in Iraq. The term "jihadi," as it is used here, refers to those Muslims who wage war against those they perceive to be the enemies of Islam (most Muslims use the word "jihad" to refer to an inner, spiritual struggle). Takfiri refers to those Muslims who pronounce others who claim to be part of the Islamic community to be, in fact, non-Muslims. For takfiris, these purported Muslims have been unfaithful to Islam and, because they are apostates, it is legal to kill them. "Al-Qaeda central"—which was Bin Laden's organization—is jihadi in the former sense but not takfiri.

The first incarnation of the jihadi/takfiri movement in Iraq, al-Tawhid wal-Jihad, was founded by Abu Musab al-Zarqawi upon his return from Afghanistan in the 1990s (*tawhid* is an Arabic term referring to the fact that "there is no God but God"—the foundation of Islam). Al-Zarqawi's fame derives from his campaign against American forces occupying Iraq. Nevertheless, al-Zarqawi was not an Iraqi: as his name denotes, he came from Zarqa in Jordan. Over the course of the fight against the Americans, al-Tawhid wal-Jihad evolved as it took on alliances with other jihadi groups, with non-jihadi groups, and as it separated from groups with which it had been aligned. The result was "al-Qaeda in Iraq," which had strained relations with al-Qaeda central. These strains were caused by the same factors that later created strains between IS and al-Qaeda central. As a takfiri, Zarqawi waged war on Shi'is as well as on the Americans, believing that the former had deviated from true Islam.

In 2006, al-Zarqawi masterminded the destruction of the Golden Mosque in Samarra, a shrine Shi'is consider sacred. Al-Zarqawi believed that the destruction would trigger Shi'i retaliation against Iraq's Sunni community, then further bloodletting between the two communities. Over time, he believed, the Sunni community would mobilize, become radicalized, and join his jihadi/takfiri campaign. Al-Zarqawi's strategy earned him a harsh rebuke from al-Qaeda central.

What this demonstrates is a long-term problem al-Qaeda central has had with its affiliates and groups which adopt its name. Al-Qaeda has always been extraordinarily weak on organization and extraordinarily strong on ideology, which is the glue that holds the organization together. The ideology of al-Qaeda can be broken down into two parts: First, the Islamic world is at war with a transnational Crusader-Zionist conspiracy and it is that conspiracy—the "far enemy"—and not the individual despots who rule the Muslim world—the "near enemy"—that is Islam's true enemy and which should be the target of al-Qaeda's jihad. To wage this jihad, al-Qaeda set out to establish temporary emirates in frontier zones from which it could "vex and exhaust" the far enemy. Second, al-Qaeda opposes the state system imposed by the Crusader-Zionist conspiracy on the Islamic world. State boundaries are to be ignored, if not eliminated. What would happen next has never been made clear—al-Qaeda has always been more definitive about what it is against than what it is for. These two points, then, are the foundation for the al-Qaeda philosophy.

They may have inspired the head of IS, Abu Bakr al-Baghdadi, but do not guide him.

We do not know much about al-Baghdadi. We know his name is a lie—he was not born in Baghdad, as his name denotes, but rather in Samarra. We know he was born in 1971 and has some sort of degree from Baghdad University. We also know he was imprisoned by the Americans in Camp Bucca in Iraq. It may have been there that he was radicalized, or perhaps upon making the acquaintance of al-Zarqawi.

Over time, al-Qaeda in Iraq evolved into the Islamic State of Iraq, which, in turn, evolved into the Islamic State of Iraq and Syria. This took place in 2013 when Baghdadi claimed that Jabhat al-Nusra, was, in fact, part of his organization. This was unacceptable to the head of Jabhat al-Nusra, Abu Muhammad al-Jawlani. Al-Jawlani took the dispute to Ayman al-Zawahiri, leader of al-Qaeda central, who ruled in his favor. Al-Zawahiri declared Jabhat al-Nusra to be the true al-Qaeda affiliate in Syria and ordered al-Baghdadi to return to Iraq. When al-Baghdadi refused, al-Zawahiri severed ties with him and his organization.

If any of this mattered to al-Baghdadi he did not let on. As a matter of fact, it seemed from his actions that al-Baghdadi was challenging al-Qaeda central for leadership of the jihadi movement. In July 2014 he launched a lightning military campaign, seizing Iraq's second largest city Mosul and threatening Baghdad. Soon thereafter, he declared the territory under his control, which stretched from Raqqa in north central Syria to the outskirts of Baghdad, a caliphate with himself as caliph. In other words, he declared himself the head of the global Islamic community and demanded fealty from it.

Some experts have said that al-Baghdadi represents the next stage in the evolution of al-Qaeda, al-Qaeda's strategy, and al-Qaeda's ideology. Al-Baghdadi certainly agrees with al-Qaeda that state boundaries are of no importance. His caliphate, for example, includes both parts of Syria and Iraq. Nevertheless, he has deviated from the al-Qaeda line by establishing a caliphate in the first place and by declaring himself caliph, moves that have split the jihadi community. On whose authority did al-Baghdadi, an unknown, become leader of the global Islamic community? In addition, many felt that al-Baghdadi had jumped the gun in declaring a caliphate. Without the establishment of emirates throughout the Muslim world to weaken the far enemy over the long haul, the enemies of Islam would simply crush it.

Besides doctrinal squabbles that have weakened al-Baghdadi's position within the movement, IS faces multiple other problems. Its enforcement of a strict interpretation of Islamic law—from the veiling of women to the prohibition of alcohol and cigarettes to the use of strict Islamic punishments and even crucifixions—has made IS extremely unpopular wherever it has established itself in Syria. When other factions of the opposition have seized towns from IS control, they are often greeted as liberators. Even the al-Qaeda affiliate Jabhat al-Nusra has taken a more relaxed stance on personal matters, to the point of allowing women who are unveiled to walk the streets of Raqqa when that group controlled the city. (The fact that Jabhat al-Nusra is composed predominantly of Syrians as opposed to IS's mostly foreign fighters might have contributed to their greater tolerance for local custom.)

In addition, although IS demonstrated that it is capable of dramatic military moves, it has only been able to conquer the territory it did because of aid from two unlikely sources. First, there were former Iraqi soldiers and their officers who had fought under Saddam Hussein and who played an outsized role in planning and carrying out the July 2014 campaign. A coalition made up of jihadis and those who had hunted them down could not last and, indeed, within a few weeks of the capture of Mosul there were reports of fighting between the two groups.

The second unlikely source of aid for IS was the unpopular prime minister of Iraq, Nouri al-Maliki. Because of his anti-Sunni policies and the corruption that marked his rule, not only did al-Maliki's army simply melt away when IS attacked Mosul, IS found allies among alienated Sunni tribes. In other words, it was not that IS was so strong, it was that it faced little opposition. But by making the gains it did, IS was then confronted by a Shi'i community with its back against the wall, a Sunni population repulsed by the harshness of IS rule, and an international coalition committed to "degrade and destroy" the organization.

Three other problems plague IS as well. First, it is fighting on multiple fronts. In Syria, it is battling most of the rest of the opposition movement, and by August 2014 it began to fight pitched battles with government forces. In Iraq, it confronts Shi'i militias on its southern flank and Kurdish militias to its north. Second, it is a relatively small organization scattered throughout a huge area. The Americans used 80,000 troops in its initial invasion of Iraq in 2003 and were still unable to control the country. IS will never be able to recruit a force of that size. Finally, we should not forget the ease with which the French ousted similar groups from Timbuktu and other areas in northern Mali in 2013. As battle-hardened as the press claims them to be, groups like IS are no match for a professional army.

Have Syria's Kurds participated in the uprising?

Rounding out the opposition is a group that might not even be in the opposition: the Kurdish Democratic Union Party (PYD), which claims to represent Syria's 2 million Kurds—about one-tenth of Syria's population—and which carved out a territorial homeland it calls "Rojava" (Western Kurdistan) in Syria's north. Founded in 2003, the PYD is actually the Syrian branch of the Kurdistan Workers Party (PKK), which has been fighting the Turkish government, much to the delight of the Syrian regime, since 1978. Although the PYD supported the Kurdish rebellion against the regime in 2004, rumors circulated by the rival Kurdistan Democratic Party maintain that it is actually working with the regime. The Syrian government did not resist the PYD's takeover of government installations (although this may have been because the regime was concentrating on battles further west), and the PYD's main actions before the emergence of IS was fighting FSA and Islamist militias in its territory. When IS emerged, it had its hands full protecting Kurds and their territory.

Whether the PYD is a wolf in sheep's clothing or the real deal, one thing is certain: If either the regime or the opposition wins a decisive victory, Rojava's days are numbered. Eastern Rojava is where the oil is.

What assistance has the Friends of Syria provided?

As in the case of Bahrain, foreign powers will likely prove critical in determining the outcome of the conflict in Syria. And as in the case of Bahrain, it is more likely that foreign assistance will prove critical in saving the regime from its opponents. It is unlikely, however, that foreign assistance will enable the regime to wipe out the opposition or regain control over the entirety of Syria.

Assistance to the rebels has come in three forms: diplomatic, humanitarian, and military. In terms of diplomacy, the Friends of Syria has recognized the Syrian National Coalition as the legitimate government of Syria. This entitles the coalition to diplomatic representation in more than one hundred countries and symbolically snatches the diplomatic high ground from the Assad government (which Secretary of State Hillary Clinton proclaimed had "lost legitimacy" in July 2011). Otherwise, recognition has had little impact on the conflict. There has been no change of representation at the United Nations, for example, nor has calling the Assad regime illegitimate prevented the United States from endorsing talks with it about removing chemical weapons from Syrian soil—talks which placed the so-called illegitimate regime on an equal footing with others at the bargaining table.

The need for humanitarian assistance is immense, both for Syrians trapped in towns and districts cut off from the outside world by regular and irregular government forces, for the internally displaced, and for refugees who have flooded into sprawling camps in neighboring countries. At a donors' conference held under the auspices of the United Nations in early 2014, UN secretary general Ban Ki-moon announced that Syrians required $6.5 billion in aid. Western nations and Gulf states, among others, immediately announced plans to donate about one-third of that (at the time the United States, the largest donor, had already donated about $1.3 billion), but in the past the your-check-is-in-the-mail syndrome has hampered fundraising and aid distribution efforts.

The regime has not made it any easier for Syrians inside the country to receive outside assistance either. It has set up numerous roadblocks, including where such aid might go, the types of aid it would permit donors to dispense, and how it is to be distributed. Whereas international aid agencies want access to areas which have been blockaded by the government and which are in desperate need of food and water, the regime continuously stipulates that aid recipients must leave those areas to gain assistance—thus removing them from their homes, exposing them to retribution, depopulating rebel strongholds, and exposing the rebels who remain behind to withering bombardment from artillery and the air.

Opposition forces fighting in Syria are most concerned about obtaining military assistance, and while such assistance has been forthcoming, rebels complain that their benefactors have been stingy with the weapon systems they need the most—such as antiaircraft guns and so-called MANPADS (man-portable air-defense systems, or shoulder-launched surface-to-air missiles). While there are reports that such weapons have been seen in rebel hands, and while Qatar and Saudi Arabia appear less squeamish about sending heavier and more advanced weapons to the opposition, before the emergence of IS the West had numerous reasons to keep their military assistance to light weapons and training.

MANPADS were decisive in turning the tide of battle in Afghanistan after the Soviet invasion of that unfortunate country in 1979. They were used by the Afghan resistance, resulting in the empowerment of the Taliban, the rise of al-Qaeda, and 9/11. No one wants to repeat that mistake. As for funneling MANPADS through the SMC and FSA, these groups have proved not only to be feckless, but are prone to infighting and are increasingly inconsequential.

Just as important, the Friends of Syria are not all on the same page when it comes to the reasons for arming the opposition. The West—and the United States in particular—fears an all-out opposition victory, particularly since it realizes that, at least at the present time, Jabhat al-Nusra, the Islamic Front, and IS wield far more power than the SMC and the Syrian National Coalition.

Hence, during the summer of 2013, when it appeared that Obama might take military action against the Syrian regime because the regime blatantly crossed his self-imposed "red line" by using chemical weapons, he ruled out regime change as a goal. Instead, the plan was to "degrade" the Syrian army. The reason? The regime had the momentum on the ground and rather than going all out as in Libya, the Obama administration wanted to restore a battlefield stalemate. In the Obama team's fevered imagination, this would open the door for the negotiated settlement discussed earlier and ensure the worst elements of the opposition would be nowhere near the corridors of power. And if during a stalemate Iran and Hizbullah would bleed a bit more, so much the better.

How have foreign powers intervened on the side of the Syrian government?

The main actors in the pro-regime camp are Iran, Hizbullah, and Russia. Although rulers of Syria and Iran are both Shi'is

(Alawites were acknowledged as part of the broader Shi'i community in 1974), the Iranian-Syrian alliance has nothing to do with shared religious affiliation or ideology. The Iranian-Syrian alliance began in 1981 during the Iran–Iraq war, when, in a brilliant strategic move, Hafez al-Assad became the only Arab leader to side with Iran. All of a sudden a medium-sized state with a weak economy became an important regional player as both Iraq's allies and Iran courted its favor, offering Syria political and financial inducements. The Iranians, recognizing a propaganda coup when they saw one, were particularly generous, offering Syria discounted oil and debt relief.

The current alliance with Iran has bolstered Syria's anti-imperialist reputation and increased the price it could demand from the West in exchange for making peace with Israel. And the Syria connection enables Iran to earn the cachet of a regional power whose field of operations stretches from the Mediterranean to the Gulf. Thus, Iran provides the Syrian regime with intelligence and has sent advisors who have instructed the Syrian military on tactics and on controlling cyberspace (which the Iranians perfected putting down their own antigovernment protests—the "Green Revolution" of 2009). It has assisted and supplied weapons to paramilitary units such as the shabiha and the popular committees. It has established an air-bridge that resupplies the Syrian army with ammunition, weapons, and even refurbished attack helicopters. And, according to reports, Iran may have sent anywhere from hundreds to thousands of combat troops to assist the Syrian regime—a charge denied by the Iranian government.

The fact that Hizbullah is deploying combat forces in Syria is, on the other hand, undeniable. Hizbullah has a huge stake in ensuring the survival of the Syrian regime. Syria provides a vital supply route that stretches from Iran to Lebanon, assuring a steady resupply of arms and equipment to a militia that has repeatedly come into conflict with Israel. Because it is itself a popular militia, Hizbullah possesses a level of expertise vital to the training of the pro-regime popular committees that protect Alawite and Shi'i villages in Syria. And unlike Iranians, members of Hizbullah have the added advantage of speaking Arabic. Hizbullah fighters were also instrumental in recapturing the town of al-Qusayr from the rebels in spring 2013. The town is strategically located near the Lebanese border, and its capture by rebel forces not only enabled them to maintain a vital route to smuggle in weapons and fighters from Lebanon and resupply rebel units to the north, but to cut the link between Damascus and Homs and regime strongholds on the coast.

The final element in the pro-regime camp is Russia. Like Iran, Russia provides Syria with weapons (as of 2014, Russia had contracted for close to $5 billion worth of arms to sell to the Syrian government), and like Iran and Hizbullah Russian advisers work closely with the Syrian military. But Russia's most important contribution to the Syrian regime's war effort has been providing the regime with diplomatic cover.

Russia has blocked numerous security council resolutions condemning actions taken by the Syrian regime, came up with the plan to remove chemical weapons from Syria (thereby making the debate in the United States about taking possible military action to punish Syria for their use moot), and supported the Syrian position during the ill-fated negotiations between the Syrian government and the opposition in early 2014. And because of Russia's support for the Syrian regime there is no chance that the United Nations will invoke a Chapter VII Resolution permitting member states to take military action against Syria on the basis of "threats to the peace, breaches of the peace, or acts of aggression"—the only justification recognized by international law for military intervention in a civil war and one which provided the basis for NATO's intervention in Libya.

How has the uprising affected Syrians and Syrian society?

The third anniversary of the Syrian uprising—March 2014—was as good a time as any to stand back and assess the impact the uprising has had on the lives of Syrians and on the Syrian social fabric. The statistics are grim. According to the Syrian Observatory for Human Rights, the death toll was at least 162,000 and might have run as high as 230,000. These statistics include 54,000 civilians, 42,700 rebel fighters, 62,800 pro-Assad Syrian fighters, more than 350 members of Hizbullah, and six hundred other foreign Shi'i fighters. In addition, the government had "disappeared" about 18,000 while rebel forces had detained or kidnapped about 8,000. In its 2013 report, Amnesty International added more dismal news: both sides had deliberately targeted journalists and committed battlefield executions, government forces targeted medical personnel who had come to the assistance of civilians, and at least 550 people (including children) died while in the custody of the government (the use of torture by both sides was commonplace).

On the third anniversary of the uprising, the number of refugees was enormous: between 2.5 and 3 million who sought shelter in neighboring countries and perhaps as many as six million Syrians internally displaced. This means that upwards of 40 percent of Syrians had fled their homes. Displacement only added to the humanitarian nightmare, creating a public health disaster and fostering the spread of diseases such as typhoid and reintroducing others such as polio. Polio had been eradicated in Syria before the beginning of the uprising. In fact, according to the World Health Organization, in 2010 polio had existed in only three countries in the world: Nigeria, Afghanistan, and Pakistan. In all likelihood, it was reintroduced to Syria by foreign fighters of the al-Qaeda variety.

Polio is a disease commonly associated with children, and by March 2014 that segment of the population had been particularly hard hit. About half of all refugees were children, who, like the children trapped in the war zones, mostly went without schooling and were denied access to regular medical care and immunizations. According to one poll conducted in a refugee camp, three out of four children there had lost a loved one and about half of them suffered from post-traumatic stress disorder or depression.

Then there is the fraying of the social fabric. The uprising transformed the physical face of Syria and with it the ties that had bound communities together. During the first three years of the uprising, fighting destroyed about one-third of the housing stock in the country and reduced entire neighborhoods to rubble. And both sides, particularly the government, engaged in what can only be described as sectarian cleansing. Here is how one activist described Homs three years into the uprising:

> Once a thriving city of approximately 700,000, [Homs] is today a broken ruin. The regime loyalist Alawi-majority districts are today the only areas of the city where normal life continues. Regime bombs have fallen relentlessly every day on the rest of the city, destroying apartment buildings, shops, and historic mosques. Entire districts, such as Khalidiya, Baba Amr, Jourat al Shiah, Bayada and Warsha have been emptied of their inhabitants and completely destroyed. Many of Homs's residents have fled from the centre of the city to the outer suburbs, such as Wa'r, which has taken in at least 200,000 refugees and is completely surrounded by the regime. Others are now outside the city or outside the country. In the Old City, not a single building remains intact and the siege on the inhabitants was complete and total. . . . No food was allowed to enter—starvation and deaths from treatable injuries were the norm. Residents had to bring in their food from under the sewers to avoid starvation.[7]

Although Sunnis, Alawites, and Christians might have harbored negative attitudes about members of other communities before the uprising, a public civility had characterized their interrelationship. That public civility, which was fostered by Sunnis, Alawites, and Christians living in close proximity, frequenting the same markets and coffeehouses, passing by each other on the sidewalks, and sharing public transportation, is now gone, as Syrians increasingly come to inhabit segregated spaces separated by walls and no man's lands. So long as Syria remains informally partitioned, that segregation will continue and broaden. In the unlikely event of a political settlement, minorities will demand written guarantees defining their rights, particularly their right to proportional representation in governance. This will inscribe sectarianism into the political process on a permanent basis, à la Lebanon. In all likelihood, a sectarianized Syria is here to stay.

How has the Syrian uprising affected Syria's neighbors?

Syria abuts Turkey, Iraq, Jordan, Israel, and Lebanon and its uprising has affected its neighbors in a number of ways. There is, for example, the threat that one or more might be pulled directly into the fighting: Israel has launched attacks on convoys and installations that appeared to threaten it directly or, through the transfer of weapons and materiel to Hizbullah, indirectly. In one of multiple incidents, Turkey and Syria engaged in an artillery duel after the Syrian army shelled a village on the Turkish side of the border in 2012. Similar incidents involved Jordan and Iraq. Sometimes deliberate or accidental Syrian army provocations precipitated them; sometimes it was armed gangs attempting to infiltrate Jordan or Iraq from Syria. And, of course, IS, spawned in Syria, has made much of Iraq into a war zone, reignited Iraq's Kurdish question, and has sparked the mass exodus of minorities to safer havens both inside the country and abroad.

Which brings us to two other effects of the Syrian uprising on the region: the flight of refugees from Syria, which has placed an enormous strain on the resources of neighboring states, and the export of Syria's sectarian troubles to those states.

In September 2014, there were more than 3 million refugees living outside the country registered with the office of the United Nations High Commissioner for Refugees. The largest number were in Lebanon (more than one million), followed by Turkey (about 850,000) and Jordan (more than 600,000). A smaller number of refugees lived in troubled Iraq (a little over 200,000) and distant Egypt and North Africa (around 140,000). To get a sense of what the influx of refugees means, take the (admittedly extreme) case of Lebanon, a country which, in normal times, had a population of 4.4 million. Syrian refugees thus make up approximately 23 percent of Lebanon's inhabitants. The equivalent number of refugees in the case of the United States would be more than 73 million. In 2013 the United States admitted a record number of refugees: seventy thousand. At the time, America's GDP was more than four hundred times that of Lebanon's.

By the beginning of 2014, the Jordanian government claimed to have spent $1.7 billion dollars for refugee assistance; the Turks, 2 billion. And the World Bank predicted Lebanon would incur about $7.5 billion in losses on account of the presence of refugees. While the international community picks up some of the tab, the burden for providing municipal services (such as lighting and road building), healthcare, educational services, and the construction of infrastructure necessary for delivering clean water falls heavily on host countries. And there are other burdens as well. The influx of refugees not living in camps drives up real estate prices, contributes to inflation, and creates tensions with local populations who fear that refugees entering the job market threaten their livelihoods (although in reality most who find jobs work as unskilled laborers, doing things citizens of their host countries consider menial).

The uprising in Syria created a unique refugee problem for Iraq. In addition to hosting Syrians, Iraq also found itself hosting Iraqi refugees who had fled to Syria with the onset of sectarian conflict in Iraq after the American invasion and occupation and returned to avoid the same dangers in their place of refuge. They are called Iraq's "doubly-displaced." With Iraq once again a war zone, it is apparent their travails have not ended.

The spillover effect of Syria's sectarian conflict has mainly affected states with significant histories of sectarian strife—Lebanon and Iraq—but it has affected Turkey as well. In Lebanon, 2013 was payback time for Hizbullah's decision to stand with and fight for the Assad regime. Militant (Sunni) Islamists from Syria followed Hizbullah fighters back to Lebanon, attacking them and their offices so often that the fighters had to set up their own "popular committees" to protect their home towns and neighborhoods. In the coastal city of Tripoli, Sunni and Shi'i gangs—the former supporting the Syrian opposition, the latter the government—clashed on an almost weekly basis. Syrian army deserters found sanctuary in the predominantly Sunni northern border area of Lebanon where they threatened Hizbullah's forces in Syria from the rear and where they, too, have clashed with local Shi'is and Hizbullah supporters. Tensions in Lebanon rose so high that the government postponed the 2013 parliamentary elections, fearing an escalation in violence that would accompany the campaign and either losses or gains by Hizbullah's electoral wing.

In 2013 Iraq faced its worst sectarian crisis since 2008 for two reasons. First, the Syrian–Iraqi border is porous, allowing militant (Sunni) Islamists freedom of movement across wide, unpoliced terrain, sometimes fighting against regime forces on the Syrian side of the border, sometimes fighting against the Shi'i-dominated Iraqi government of Nouri al-Maliki on the other side. In addition, the Sunni Arab population of Iraq, concentrated in the area to the north and west of Baghdad, are a minority (Shi'is make up 60–65% of the population of Iraq) and complain of discrimination and abuse by the government. They found inspiration in the actions of their coreligionists in Syria. In the winter of 2013, they began mounting a series of antigovernment demonstrations which led Iraqis down the same path previously trod by Syrians: the government met the protests with repression (calling its leaders former supporters of Saddam Hussein), which moved Sunni tribal leaders to form a tribal army, which led to the militarization of what had begun as peaceful protests, replete with car bombings and assassinations. Hence, the support many gave to IS in the immediate aftermath of its military foray into Iraq.

One does not usually associate Turkey with sectarian problems (it is most noted for its problems with its Kurdish minority), but it, too, has experienced a rise in sectarian tensions as a result of the Syrian uprising. Two minority groups in particular have come to resent the Turkish government's anti-Assad stance, its playing footsie with Sunni extremists in Syria, and the influx of mostly Sunni refugees from Syria into the areas they inhabit: Turkish Alevis, who make up 10–20 percent of the population, and Alawites, who are mainly of Arab descent with strong ties to their Syrian coreligionists (and yes, their names are not the only difference between the two groups). Beginning in 2013, protests and clashes between members of both communities and police, as well as bombings heightened tensions in southern Turkey. And to top matters off, Syrian Kurds fleeing IS began arriving in Turkey in droves in late September 2014.

Why is a negotiated settlement for Syria improbable?

The most serious attempt to bring the two sides in the Syrian conflict together took place at the 2014 Geneva II peace talks. The talks were based on the Geneva Communiqué which had been signed in 2012 at a meeting that included representatives of the United Nations, the Arab League, the European Union, and nine governments including the United States and

Russia. The communiqué outlined steps to be taken to establish a transitional government "formed on the basis of mutual consent."

Geneva II was a non-starter. Much of the opposition stayed away, the two sides refused to engage with each other directly, there was endless wrangling over procedural issues and accusations of bad faith and, perhaps most importantly, no clear consensus on the meaning of the Geneva Communiqué. The United States and the opposition asserted that any transitional government could not include Bashar al-Assad; the government and its Russian ally asserted that there was no such stipulation in the communiqué (they were, in fact, correct, although the communiqué did stipulate that both sides had to agree on the transitional government's members). After an opposition spokesman commented that no one in the regime with blood on his hands could be part of a transitional government, a reporter asked him who from the government could. The spokesman shrugged and said that maybe there was a government chauffeur who fit the bill. In the end, the talks failed because the regime was not interested and the opposition would not have been able to deliver even if it had been.

As discussed earlier, the three possible endgame scenarios for the Syrian conflict are total victory for the regime, total victory for the opposition, or protracted stalemate. The last case, which is the most probable, would lead to what UN and Arab League special envoy to Syria Lakhdar Brahimi called the "Somalization" of Syria (Brahimi, who oversaw the Geneva II debacle, resigned from his position in disgust in May 2014 after Bashar al-Assad had himself reelected president). In other words, Syria would still have a seat at the United Nations and other international councils, but its territory would be parceled out among the government and its supporters, various armed militias, and perhaps the Kurds, each of which would jealously guard its domain and enviously eye the domains of others.

A negotiated settlement is only possible if two conditions are met. First, both the regime and the most important components of the opposition would have to view the battlefield situation as hopelessly deadlocked, and they would have to do so simultaneously. After all, if there was a chance your side might achieve total victory, why bother to attempt to reach a compromise through negotiations? At the same time, if your side were losing, what leverage would you have to bring the other side to the negotiating table? (One major fly in the ointment: neither Jabhat al-Nusra nor IS is interested in negotiating under any conditions and would be more than happy to act as spoilers.)

The second condition that has to be fulfilled to reach a negotiated settlement is that every major outside player—the United States and other Western states, Saudi Arabia, Turkey, Russia, Iran, and others—would also have to come to the conclusion—again simultaneously—that there was no chance their clients could score a victory on the battlefield and that, in the big scheme of things, the battle for Syria was just not worth the cost. Otherwise, when your side is down why not try to restore its fortunes by pumping in more supplies, heavier and more lethal weapons, cash, and perhaps fresh recruits?

All this being said, there is one possibility, albeit farfetched, that might enable a negotiated settlement to prevail. So far, the United States and its allies have been acting as if Syria were a chess game where a win for one side on a two-dimensional board means a loss for the other. Why not start playing three-dimensional chess? In other words, why treat Syria as a separate problem to be solved in isolation? Why not complicate the Syria problem by making it one of a number of issues to be brought to the table at the same time? This would increase the number of possible trade-offs and compromises, allow governments to save face through reciprocal exchanges, and make grand bargains possible.

For example, Iran has a stake in Syria. But Iran also has nuclear aspirations and a desire to end international sanctions that have been applied against it because of its pursuit of those aspirations. Iran also has interests which it wants to protect in Iraq, Afghanistan, Lebanon, the Gulf, etc. And, probably most important, Iran wants a seat at the grown-up's table—that is, it wants recognition that it is an important regional player. Russia presents a similar case. Backing Syrian hardliners for such trifles as arms deals, port facilities at Tartus, and bragging rights for standing up to the United States pale in comparison with the possibility of concessions by the international community on Crimea/Ukraine, the end to international sanctions for its role there, keeping the spigots turned on for natural gas destined for Europe, and recognition of Russia's special relationship with its southern frontier (the "near abroad"). And so long as Syria festers, Russia, like the rest of the world, faces an al-Qaeda resurgence and bigger headaches in Chechnya.

5

THE REGIONAL AND GLOBAL MEANINGS OF THE ARAB UPRISINGS

Did the Arab monarchies dodge the bullet during the uprisings?

There are more monarchies in the Arab world (eight) than in any other region, save Europe (in which there are twelve, if one includes the Vatican): Morocco, Jordan, Saudi Arabia, Kuwait, Bahrain, Oman, Qatar, and the United Arab Emirates. If one counts the number of monarchies in which kings or queens rule as well as reign, no other region of the world even comes close.

The reason for this has nothing to do with anything intrinsic to the region—tradition or tribalism or Islam. Rather, the reason is that imperialist powers created most of the monarchies and protected all of them when they were threatened. During the nineteenth century, the British chose kings from among the leading families of what would become Kuwait, Qatar, the UAE (called the Trucial States before their independence in 1971 because they pledged a "perpetual maritime truce" in the Gulf) who would go on to found dynasties. They placed their territories, along with Bahrain, under British protection. One other Gulf state, Oman (formerly Muscat and Oman, a name that reflects the two main geographic divisions of the country), was never an official protectorate, but might as well have been, considering the level of British influence in the royal court. All this was done to maintain tranquility in the Gulf—the final stepping-stone on the route to India—and to suppress piracy and the slave trade.

Two monarchies emerged later with British assistance. The British created Trans-Jordan (later the Hashemite Kingdom of Jordan) "one Sunday afternoon with a stroke of a pen" (as Winston Churchill later wrote) by slicing their League of Nations mandate for Palestine in two, keeping that name for the part west of the Jordan River and making the part east of the river Trans-Jordan (hence, the name). They established as emir (prince) one of the sons of Sharif Hussein of Mecca, an Arabian warlord who had pledged his support for the British cause during World War I. After independence, he became Jordan's first king, while a British officer commanded the Jordanian army until 1956.

Saudi Arabia also emerged during the interwar period. Saudi Arabia owes its existence to the conquest of much of the Arabian peninsula by the family patriarch, Abdulaziz ibn Abdul Rahman al-Sa'ud, and his band of warriors, the *ikhwan* (brothers), although he, too, depended on British assistance, and his incipient state became a "veiled protectorate" of the British from 1915 to 1927. They guaranteed the integrity of its borders so long as he behaved himself and stayed away from their other protectorates on the Gulf.

The French supported monarchies in their protectorates of Morocco and Tunisia, and even saved the former when it was threatened by a republican revolt in 1921. It was, after all, easier to rule through a monarch who represented a royal house that had ruled independently since the seventeenth century and claimed descent from the family of the prophet Muhammad than it was to try to rule directly. During Morocco's struggle for independence, the nationalist movement adopted him as a national symbol. Tunisia's monarch was not so lucky—the nationalist movement abolished the monarchy soon after independence.

Foreign powers continued to intervene to preserve monarchies throughout the twentieth century, sometimes under the guise of preventing subversion (such as when Britain briefly reoccupied Jordan in 1958), sometimes simply to assure access to oil and a regional balance of power (such as when the United States put together an international coalition to dislodge Iraq from Kuwait in 1991).

Foreign powers thus created monarchies, assured their survival, or both. As a result, it would seem dynasties would not have—or need to have—an organic relationship with those they ruled. Nevertheless, the monarchies seemed to prove that they did not lack for inner resiliency during the 2010–11 wave of uprisings. While uprisings in the republics demanded the end of the regime, protests in most of the monarchies seemed to follow a different path. Two kingdoms—Qatar and the UAE—experienced no real protests at all, and protests in most of the remainder did not call for the overthrow of the regime, merely its reform. The key word here is "most." The exceptions to the rule demonstrate that there is nothing intrinsic to monarchic rule that enabled the monarchies to dodge the bullet during the season of the uprisings.

What were the protests in the monarchies like?

At the core of the protests that began in the first months of 2011 were social networking youths, such as those found in Egypt and Tunisia, whose ability to mobilize street demonstrations ranged from impressive to nonexistent. In many places, there was not a protest movement per se, but rather a number of individual protest movements made up of different groups with their own sets of grievances or demands acting simultaneously or in tandem. The relatively privileged protesters in Saudi Arabia's capital, Riyadh, for example, had a different agenda from the Shi'is in Saudi Arabia's Eastern

Province, for whom discrimination and unemployment were major concerns.

Some demands were, however, consistent. Days before the March 11 protests scheduled for Riyadh, protest organizers issued a fourteen-point manifesto entitled "Demands of the Saudi Youth for the Future of the Nation."[1] As in most other monarchies, protesters in Saudi Arabia demanded expanded economic opportunities, an end to poverty (yes, there is poverty in Saudi Arabia), democratic reform, an end to corruption, transformation of the system of government to a constitutional monarchy, greater transparency in governance, equal rights for all citizens regardless of race or sect, release of prisoners of conscience, and the like.

A number of analysts have offered reasons why protests in the monarchies tended to be more limited in scope than those in the republics and have, more often than not, demanded reform of the regime, not its overthrow. Some cite oil wealth, which allowed various monarchs to buy off their populations (the Saudis alone promised their population $130 billion in benefits). Others cite the special legitimacy that comes from generations-long dynastic rule—something a number of presidents considered but only one (Hafez al-Assad) was able to pull off. Still others cite the fact that monarchies sever executive from legislative power, enabling monarchs to float above the fray while populations vent their anger on prime ministers or parliaments. (The king of Jordan is particularly adept at this maneuver, having dismissed three different prime ministers between February 2011 and October 2012 to mollify protesters.)

A quick look at the facts shows that none of these explanations is satisfactory. Morocco and Jordan have no oil with which to buy off their oppositions. Instead of buying loyalty, the king of Morocco adroitly manipulated the opposition and bought it off with cosmetic constitutional changes (such as changing his title and making Berber an official language), thereby taking the wind out of the sails of the protest movement. And if oil wealth ensures or even contributes to stability, how would one explain Libya?

Three Arab republics—the Comoros (islands off the east coast of Africa), Lebanon, and Somalia—had, like Qatar and the UAE, neither a significant protest movement nor an uprising, while Bahrain had an uprising replete with calls for ending the monarchy (as did Jordan in November 2012, when no one was looking). This undercuts the argument that dynastic rule somehow endows kings with legitimacy presidents lack.

Finally, while parliaments in Jordan and Kuwait can be rough and tumble, on whom could the Saudi king shift blame for bad times? Saudi Arabia, a wholly owned subsidiary of the al-Sa'ud family, lacks a true parliament and the prime minister is—the king.

Primed by Arab Spring dreams and the optimism of the heady days in Egypt and Tunisia and ready to call it a day after the outbreak of the "last" uprising in Syria, all but the closest observers missed the violence that accompanied the protests in various monarchies. Violent protests broke out in Qatif, Saudi Arabia, in the oil-rich, Shi'i-dominated Eastern Province, when Shi'i demonstrators clashed with security personnel not just once but twice (March 2011 and January 2012).

In Jordan, protests against corruption and economic conditions began as early as January 2011 and built in size and scope, culminating in a series of nationwide protests from September through November 2012. In September and October 2012, hundreds, then thousands of Jordanians nationwide protested the removal of fuel subsidies, expanded censorship, and corruption. The king ordered the subsidies restored while the prime minister took the fall. In November, the regime again tried to lower subsidies. This time, tens of thousands took to the streets, many shouting the ubiquitous slogan of the Arab uprisings, "The people want the fall of the regime." For the second time, a monarch had become the target of popular ire.

Adding up all the factors, it appears that there is no basis to differentiate the experiences of the monarchies with popular unrest from the multiform experiences of the republics. No monarchic exceptionalism exists.

What role have the Gulf monarchies played in uprisings elsewhere?

One of the more interesting aspects of the uprisings has been the transformation of the Gulf countries—particularly Saudi Arabia, Qatar, and the UAE—from political, cultural, and diplomatic backwaters to vital players not only in the uprisings but in regional politics as a whole.

Qatar started things off. The Qatar-based news service, *al-Jazeera*, spread the news of the Tunisian and Egyptian uprisings well beyond those countries, ensuring copycat Days of Rage in a number of places. Unfortunately, its coverage of Egypt during and after Morsi's presidential tenure (which the king of Qatar supported) and of Syria (where it was hardly fair and balanced because of his hatred of the Assad regime) tarnished its reputation, perhaps irreversibly. Qatar sent troops to fight in Libya and, along with the UAE, deployed its air force there.

Saudi Arabia was instrumental in brokering the deal that forced Ali Abdullah Saleh from power in Yemen and, along with the UAE, sent forces into Bahrain to put down that uprising. It even put out feelers to integrate Morocco and Jordan into the Saudi-dominated GCC, which would have given the council regional breadth.

Both Qatar and Saudi Arabia have supported the Syrian opposition, although the groups they have supported differ. Until 2014, Qatar was the largest supplier of aid to the opposition—estimated at $3 billion in the first two years of the uprising alone. Now the largest supplier is Saudi Arabia, which pioneered novel ways of getting around the European Union's arms embargo to Syria. For example, it worked secretly with the United States and Britain to finance the purchase of weapons from Croatia left over from the Yugoslav civil war. And this points to the most lethal weapon in the Gulf States' arsenal: their wealth.

In 2012, Saudi Arabia earned $311 billion from oil sales, the UAE $100 billion, Kuwait $88 billion, and Qatar $55 billion. Lest one feel sympathy for Qatar's poor showing on this list, they should remember that in 2014 there were fewer than 300,000 Qatari citizens (who lived among more than 1.5 million guest workers). The Gulf States have a lot of money to spend winning friends and influencing people. Qatar financed Egypt under Morsi to the tune of $8 billion. No friends of Morsi or the Muslim Brotherhood, Saudi Arabia, Kuwait, and the UAE did better, paying his military successors $12 billion.

Why have the Gulf monarchies played such a prominent role in the uprisings?

While uprisings taking place in their backyard alone should have awakened the Gulf states from their lethargy, there were more serious factors lurking in the background that stirred them into action. At the top of the list is the perception held by the Saudis and others that under Obama the United States lacked resolve when it came to Middle East issues. The Saudis were bitterly disappointed when the Obama administration did not do more to shore up Mubarak during his waning days, although just what the United States could have done is unclear. (Besides, the United States *did* stick by Mubarak, almost until the bitter end, before it turned to Mubarak's hand-picked vice president, Omar Suleiman, to form a transitional government. The United States neither threw Mubarak under a bus nor rushed to embrace the opposition.) The Saudis also resented America's attempt to reach out to the Morsi regime and decried what can be at best described as American ambivalence when a democratically elected president was overthrown by a coup d'état.

Then there is Syria. Since the beginning, the Saudis have pushed the United States to do more in Syria, but for them the *pièce de résistance* was the debacle that took place in the summer of 2013. Having declared the use of chemical weapons by the regime a red line that it could cross only at its peril, the regime used them anyway. After threatening force, Obama then announced air strikes would be up to Congress, then backed down entirely and grasped at a Russian plan for international inspections and the removal and destruction of the weapons. The Saudis were apoplectic and, in the wake of the incident, bolstered their aid to the opposition.

Finally, the American outreach to Iran, including the American-initiated interim nuclear deal—as tentative and shaky as it was—represents for the Saudis both the height of betrayal and another opportunity to trot out the Neville Chamberlain/Munich analogy. In exchange for a short-term freeze on some of Iran's nuclear ambitions, the United States and its partners lifted some of the economic sanctions they had imposed on that country. This was to be the start of a process whose end would be a compromise on the nuclear issue and a total lifting of sanctions. Instead of negotiations, the Saudis would have preferred American airstrikes to eliminate the threat of an Iran equipped with nuclear weapons.

This brings us to the second reason the Gulf states have taken the initiative in regional politics: the perception that they are locked in a death match with Iran for regional influence. In spite of all the talk about a Sunni–Shi'i divide that will remake the future map of the Middle East, Saudi Arabia's problem with Iran is geostrategic, not religious. If it were a religious problem, how would one explain Iran's support for the Sunni Islamist Hamas movement, which controlled Gaza, to the tune of millions of dollars (before Hamas sided with the Syrian opposition), or Qatari outreach to Iran?

Saudi Arabia is a status quo power that has little interest in seeing its fortunes and room for maneuver decline at the hands of a rival regional power. Iran, on the other hand, is spoiling for a chance to reshuffle the deck, not only to strengthen its position and expand its influence, but to be taken seriously as a major player. Iran views the survival of its Syrian ally as critical to fulfilling its ambitions, and it would not mind supplementing that alliance (and its alliance with Hizbullah) with closer ties to Iraq and perhaps even Qatar. Talk about Iranian subversion in Bahrain and Yemen might have provided Saudi Arabia and its allies an excuse to intervene to determine the outcome of the uprisings in both countries, but it also reflects a deep fear of a nuclear-armed Iran dominating the region.

There is a third reason why Gulf countries have suddenly become proactive: interstate competition, particularly the competition between Qatar and Saudi Arabia.

On first view, such competition cannot but appear overblown. In terms of size, population, oil revenue, and military capabilities, there is no comparison between the two countries. But tensions between them escalated to such an extent that in March 2014 Saudi Arabia, the UAE, and Bahrain withdrew their ambassadors from Qatar. While the visit of the Qatari foreign minister to Tehran, and his suggestion that Iran could play a constructive role in negotiations about Syria, might have been the straw that broke the camel's back, the real problem between Saudi Arabia and Qatar is rival survival strategies.

After cross-border raids by the ikhwan into British-mandated Iraq in the 1920s threatened to bring down the wrath of the British Empire on the fledgling Saudi kingdom, the Saudi king needed a way to rein them in, secure Saudi Arabia as a state, and consolidate power in his own hands. He therefore deemed a change in official state doctrine, known as Wahhabism, necessary. Rather than using the strict puritanical teachings of Wahhabism to fuel warrior zeal, the retooled doctrine stipulated that obedience to the ruler and political quiescence represent true piety. And being a status-quo state made that obedience and quiescence, at home and abroad, even more imperative. Those who sought to blend Islam and politics were to be opposed, particularly if they operated in multiple countries at the same time and held the branch office that operated in the largest and most powerful Arab state—Egypt—in special esteem. Hence, the Saudi animosity toward the Muslim brotherhoods, wherever they might be.

Qatar, on the other hand, sees political Islam as practiced by the various brotherhoods and their spin-offs as the wave of the future and has decided to ride that wave. Hence Qatar's support for Morsi's government in Egypt, Ghannouchi's in Tunisia, and the Syrian Muslim Brotherhood-dominated Syrian National Council—all of which Saudi Arabia detested. And if Qatar decides to become a regional player itself—and at the same time buy itself another insurance policy by reaching out to Iran—so much the worse for its relations with Saudi Arabia.

The Saudi–Qatari rivalry should put to rest once and for all the idea that just because a state's ruler or population is Sunni or Shi'i, that state will necessarily walk in lockstep with other Sunni or Shi'i states. That being the case, the convulsions the region is currently experiencing cannot be reduced, as a number of pundits have done, to a simple Sunni/Shi'i struggle for dominance.

Is American power in the Middle East on the wane?

The Saudi (and Iranian) claim that the United States' power in the Middle East is not what it used to be has also found resonance in the media and in the halls of Congress. The United States could not or did not do anything to prevent the overthrow of allied strongmen and wields little influence in the messy Syrian situation. The Obama administration's attempts to resolve the Israeli–Palestinian conflict through negotiations were as unsuccessful as its attempts to resolve the Syria problem the same way. The optimism spawned by the Arab uprisings is long gone, some local powers (such as Saudi Arabia) feel the need to step up to the plate while others (such as Iran) gleefully smell blood in the water, and the American public is tired of waging wars in a region which they view as riddled by tribalism and ancient hatreds. Around the time Obama was considering air strikes on Syria because the regime had used chemical weapons, more Americans believed Congress was doing a good job than believed the United States should undertake another military adventure in the region.

Perception sometimes creates reality, so the perception of America's declining power in the region and globally should not be taken lightly. On the other hand, the reality that perception creates is often fleeting.

But all the talk of decline begs a question: Decline from when? When, exactly, was America's golden age in the Middle East? In 1958, when the entire Arab world seemed to have fallen under the sway of Gamal Abd al-Nasser's Pan-Arab dream and anti-imperialism? In 1967, when American diplomacy failed to prevent an Arab–Israeli war? In 1973, when the Organization of Petroleum Exporting Countries (OPEC) raised oil prices 380 percent in two months? In 1976, when Syrian forces intervened in the Lebanese civil war and remained in Lebanon for almost thirty years? In 1978–79, when a revolution in Iran, a close ally, installed the current regime? In 1983, when 241 American servicemen died after a car bomb exploded at their barracks in Beirut (after which the remainder of the contingent was withdrawn)? In 1990, when Saddam Hussein invaded Kuwait? During the countless attempts to bang Israeli and Palestinian heads together to come up with a workable peace agreement? 9/11?

Anwar al-Sadat once said he switched sides from the Soviet Union to the United States in the early 1970s because the United States "held 99% of the cards in the region." What he meant by "the cards" was America's ability to mediate the Arab–Israeli dispute by forcing Israel to disgorge the territories it occupied in the 1967 War in exchange for peace treaties with the surrounding states that wanted their territories back. The Soviets, who had broken relations with Israel, could not help him.

For Sadat, Israel and those surrounding states comprised the extent of the region in which he was interested. Sadat got his land back, but in spite of countless American attempts only one other treaty between Israel and a neighbor was signed and ratified. Such was the extent of the vaunted American power.

After more than a decade fighting two wars in the region to no avail, Americans—with the possible exception of those who got us into them—have been gun-shy about undertaking a third (although it appears they got it anyway). But warmaking is not the only criterion by which power might be measured. Power is also the ability to influence by non-lethal means. So as far as the United States being a waning power is concerned, here are two things to consider: First, during the uprisings protesters throughout the Arab world went out on the streets demanding human and democratic rights—two values the United States had been promoting—sometimes cynically, sometimes sincerely—in every international venue for close to four decades. And no matter how much pain it might cause, the only formula for economic recovery in the Arab world currently on the table is neoliberalism, which might as well come with the label "made in America."

How has the United States reacted to the Arab uprisings?

According to inside accounts, when Barack Obama became president in 2009 the prevailing view among his foreign policy staff was that the United States had expended far too much time and effort on Middle East issues during the administration of George W. Bush and far too little time and effort on Asia, which, they believed, would be the epicenter of global competition in the twenty-first century. The Obama administration's much vaunted attempt to "pivot to Asia" was one of the reasons Obama finalized the withdrawal of American troops from Iraq and the drawdown of troops from Afghanistan. This was also in part why he used so much political capital in the early days of his administration trying to bring about a quick resolution to the interminable Israeli–Palestinian conflict. Once the conflict was resolved, Obama believed, other pieces of the Middle East puzzle would simply fall into place and the United States could turn its attention to more pressing matters.

Events in the Arab world overtook the refocus of American policy, and although Obama and top policymakers may not have foreseen the Tunisian uprising and those that followed, they were not totally unprepared either. Like some political scientists studying the Arab world, they saw, in general terms, the problems that might arise in the area as a result of aging autocrats and a series of succession crises. In August 2010, four months before the outbreak of the first uprising, Obama circulated a memorandum entitled "Political Reform in the Middle East and North Africa" to his top civilian and military advisors.[2] It noted a recent uptick in both unrest and repression in the region, which could imperil American interests there: "Our regional and international credibility will be undermined if we are seen or perceived to be backing repressive regimes and ignoring the rights and aspirations of citizens." Obama ordered a response that would maintain American interests while taking into account the on-the-ground situation in each country.

Although this approach made the United States appear sometimes indecisive, sometimes hypocritical, the Obama administration consciously moved away from any all-encompassing doctrine such as the "freedom agenda" or the "you're either with us or with the terrorists" policy of the previous administration. Those policies, the Obama administration believed, had tied the hands of American policymakers and made them bend themselves out of shape in an attempt to justify any actions that deviated from the doctrine. Hence, the approach taken by Obama was based on a country-by-country assessment of policy needs and American capabilities.

Since Egypt was a close ally and the Egyptian peace treaty with Israel a centerpiece of American policy in the region, Obama felt it necessary first to support the pro-American, pro-treaty Mubarak. When Mubarak's position became untenable, the Americans switched their allegiance to his vice president, and when a president from the Muslim Brotherhood took office, the United States tried to maintain a friendly, if wary, relationship with him as well. After the army deposed Morsi, American–Egyptian relations naturally chilled, but less than a month after the coup d'état, Secretary of State John Kerry visited Cairo and opined that the military was "restoring democracy."

The chill is likely to remain. For example, in the spring of 2014 the Egyptians announced that they were diversifying their source of arms and signed a $3 billion arms deal with the Russians. The reasons for this were probably continued fallout from the purported American "embrace" of the Muslim Brotherhood (a fabrication widely believed in Egypt) and Gulf-generated prattle about American unreliability. In the end, the American–Egyptian relationship will be defined by the fact that even if the love is gone, each needs the other, particularly since the Egyptian military still relies on American-made equipment and at least some of that equipment is used to fight the American-made war on terrorism.

American interests in Yemen and Bahrain concern mainly counterterrorism and defense. Therefore, the Obama administration worked with the Saudis to ensure some sort of resolution to the uprising in the former that did not involve radical change, and looked the other way when troops from Saudi Arabia and the UAE put down the uprising in the latter. And a little over a year after that invasion and the beginning of a wave of ruthless repression, the United States resumed arms sales to the island kingdom.

Critics of the Obama administration assert that if the United States had acted earlier in Syria it might have been able to turn the tide in favor of the opposition, as it had done in Libya. But in spite of the fact that the administration maintained in public that Assad could become part of the solution rather than remain part of the problem long after he had demonstrated he could not, what exactly, was the United States supposed to do?

In all probability, the first reaction of the administration to the Syrian uprising was that a return to the status quo, with perhaps a national dialogue or two thrown in, would provide the best solution. Even though Syria was no friend of the United States and was receiving Iranian assistance, the Americans had looked the other way when the shoe was on the other foot and Saudi Arabia and the UAE came to the assistance of Bahrain's regime. And there was something to be said for a stable, if autocratic Syria that was situated in a neighborhood where any spark might set off sectarian fires in Iraq or Lebanon or even conflict with Israel. As a matter of fact, for all their anti-imperialist rhetoric, the Assads had kept the border with Israel quiet since 1973, and up until the outbreak of the uprising Syria was secretly negotiating with Israel for the return of the Golan Heights, Syrian territory the Israelis had taken in 1967.

No one in the administration could articulate such a stance in public, of course, and once the conflict became militarized in January 2012 American options diminished even further. Every time some civilian suggested further arming the opposition, setting up humanitarian safe zones in Syria, or establishing a no-fly zone over the country American generals would roll their eyes at the naiveté of amateurs. While there was no excuse for the embarrassment caused by the disappearing red line in the summer of 2013, Geneva II and a hope and a prayer was the best the United States could reach for.

The United States did get involved after ISIS morphed into IS and took control over parts of Syria and Iraq. United States' warplanes began flying missions against the Islamic State and dropped food and water to besieged communities. It also organized a multinational coalition to deal with the IS problem once and for all. Obama declared the reasons the United States had all of a sudden gone on a war footing was to address a humanitarian crisis, protect United States' assets and personnel in Iraq, and prevent the Islamic State from eventually committing acts of terrorism on United States' soil. He left the real reason unspoken, however. The Islamic State represents a threat to the regional order that the United States had spent more than half a century shoring up. And there was Saudi Arabia, Iraq's southern neighbor, to think of.

Looking back at American actions during the uprisings, there is little to make Americans feel proud. Despite decades of preaching human rights and democracy, the United States helped ensure the victory of only one opposition movement—the one in Libya. Then it abandoned that country to its own devices. In Yemen and Bahrain the United States did nothing when the powers that be ensured there would be no seat at the table for the independent opposition, and in Syria the United States views a clear victory by the opposition with as much, if not more fear than a clear victory for the government. The cruel irony of America's reaction to the uprisings is that it took place under the stewardship of a president who said, "No matter how callously defined, neither America's interests—nor the world's—are served by the denial of human aspirations,"[3] when he picked up his Nobel Peace Prize in 2009.

Did George W. Bush's "Freedom Agenda" pave the way for the Arab uprisings?

The first time the phrase "Arab Spring" appeared in print was in 2005 in the wake of a series of events—including elections in Iraq and the Cedar Revolution in Lebanon—that some commentators believed George W. Bush's "freedom agenda" had inspired. Bush had announced his freedom agenda in a speech delivered in November 2003. "Sixty years of Western nations excusing and accommodating the lack of freedom in the Middle East did nothing to make us safe—because in the long run, stability cannot be purchased at the expense of liberty," Bush declared. "As long as the Middle East remains a place where freedom does not flourish, it will remain a place of stagnation, resentment and violence ready for export."[4] The Bush administration thus announced its public commitment to "democracy promotion" in the region. Then, in the wake of the uprisings in Tunisia and Egypt, former Bush associates and their supporters in the press made what seemed to them the logical connection between then and now: the freedom agenda worked.

Others, however, have not found the connection so logical. Some recall the multiple uprisings for human rights and democracy that predated the freedom agenda by close to a quarter of a century. Others claim that the connection the Bush administration made between "democracy promotion" and the American invasion of Iraq so linked "democracy" with "American imperialism" that pro-democracy activists in the Arab world were put on the defensive rather than empowered. They also assert that after a brief flirtation with the freedom agenda, the Bush administration pretty much returned to business as usual (rhetoric aside), maintaining a cozy relationship with Mubarak, Saleh, and even Qaddafi.

Most important, there is the difference between the broad strategy the freedom agenda advocated to bring about change and the broad strategy the uprisings have applied. The freedom agenda took a top-down approach, assuming concessions by autocrats would, over time, lead to true reform. Hence, the attempts to get them to undertake electoral reform and hold free elections. Populations in the region, on the other hand, knew that no autocrat would make any concession liable to put him out of business. Thus, they took matters into their own hands.

The freedom agenda did not change the behavior of autocrats in any significant way. Its top-down strategy was misguided and proved to be a dead-end. But if the freedom agenda fell short in achieving that particular goal, it might be argued that it was not a complete failure either. It had a consequence that was unanticipated by the Bush administration. While the freedom agenda did not compel a single autocrat to see and correct the errors of his ways, when it came to defining the terms of political struggle in the region it did put the issue of human and democratic rights on the front burner. This gave encouragement to the proponents of those rights and normalized advocating for them. They, not reformed autocrats, ensured the quest for human and democratic rights would remain on the political agenda.

Have the uprisings strengthened or weakened al-Qaeda?

The year 2011 was not a good one for al-Qaeda. In early May, US Navy Seals stormed a compound in Abbottabad, Pakistan, and shot dead Osama bin Laden, al-Qaeda's mastermind. Although this event grabbed the headlines, it is debatable just how important bin Laden remained to an organization that had become one in name only. For years, a number of al-Qaeda franchises—al-Qaeda in Iraq, al-Qaeda in the Arabian Peninsula, al-Qaeda in Islamic North Africa—had operated autonomously and not always without friction. Thus, it is entirely possible that historians of the future will mark the Arab uprisings, not the assassination of bin Laden, as the milestone event for al-Qaeda in 2011.

For many observers, the outbreak of the uprisings demonstrated that al-Qaeda's message had fallen on deaf ears in the Arab world. Ideologues associated with the organization had argued for years that removing local autocrats—the "near enemy"—did not matter so long as the Crusader-Zionist conspiracy—the "far enemy"—still controlled the world and warred against Islam. Protesters in the Arab world clearly did not listen and even scored successes by taking on the near enemy.

Al-Qaedists believed that the boundaries separating Muslim states from each other were engineered by the Crusader-Zionist conspiracy to divide Muslims and keep them weak. Thus, the boundaries and the divisions they foster had to go. Although protesters in various countries found inspiration and learned from protests elsewhere in the Arab world, each uprising was a *national* uprising, targeting a specific government against which protesters held specific grievances.

Al-Qaedists believed that the Crusader-Zionist conspiracy against Islam obligates every Muslim to engage in "defensive jihad," which, for them, means armed struggle. Yet from Tunisia to Egypt to Bahrain, protesters embraced the tactic of nonviolent resistance.

Finally, al-Qaedists believed that Muslims should obey the rule of God, not the rule of man, and that true freedom lies in obedience to Islamic law and freedom from the materialism and oppression of the West. Yet among the central demands of the protesters was democratic governance—rule by the majority, not by the word of God—and respect for internationally accepted norms of human rights. These are certainly not al-Qaeda's ideals.

Over time, however, the consensus about the meaning of the uprisings for al-Qaeda shifted. Many in the Arab world came to realize that the removal of autocrats hardly guaranteed good governance, nor did it change their lives for the better. The uprisings weakened the control of some Arab governments over their territories, thus providing al-Qaeda affiliates with sanctuaries from which they might "vex and exhaust"[5] their enemies. From Tunisia to the Sinai to Syria and Iraq, affiliates, wannabes, and copycat groups proliferated, wreaked havoc on weak transitional governments, and sometimes took the lead in ongoing struggles. One even established a caliphate carved out of Syria and Iraq. Finally, uprisings in Libya, Yemen, Syria, and Bahrain seemingly confirmed al-Qaeda's core belief that victory against oppression could be won only through violence.

Perhaps, however, the consensus once again requires reevaluation. The proliferation of affiliates, wannabes, and copycat groups, and their expansion into new territories, mask a phenomenon that would have been deeply troubling to the original al-Qaeda cohort. From its inception, al-Qaeda was not big on organization. Bin Laden himself once remarked there was no such thing as al-Qaeda. The term, he claimed, merely referred to what a bunch of guys hanging out in the Afghan badlands waging jihad called their headquarters—their base (*al-qaeda* in Arabic)—a term which Westerners latched on to and endowed with substance. More important than organization was ideology—the common bond that held al-Qaeda affiliates together and united them with al-Qaeda central.

But now al-Qaeda's ideological cohesion, like the authority of al-Qaeda central, has dissipated. Various Ansar al-Sharias have taken on a local coloration, deny affiliation with al-Qaeda (in part to avoid being tainted by appearing alien), and have forsaken global jihad in favor of fighting national governments within the framework of their nations. They even call themselves by their local names—*ansar al-shari'a bi-tunis* (Ansar al-Sharia in Tunisia), *ansar al-shari'a bi-libya* (Ansar al-Sharia in Libya) to distinguish themselves from similarly named organizations outside their national borders.

And then there is the peculiar case of Jabhat al-Nusra and ISIS/IS in Syria. Not only did ISIS/IS defy al-Qaeda central by refusing to leave the struggle in Syria to Jabhat al-Nusra, its leader put himself above Ayman al-Zawahiri of al-Qaeda central by declaring himself caliph; that is, the supreme leader of the Muslim world. It also delights in sectarian violence, which al-Qaeda central has traditionally found counterproductive. For its part, Jabhat al-Nusra, an official al-Qaeda affiliate, abandoned central elements of al-Qaeda's program, asserting its struggle was in Syria alone and its aim was to overthrow Bashar al-Assad. It set aside the Islamic punishments and restrictions on personal behavior and religious practice that made ISIS/IS unpopular in the territories it had "liberated," and even fought pitched turf wars with ISIS/IS.

What, then, is al-Qaeda's current state? If one looks at al-Qaeda not as an entity but as a tendency within a broader jihadi movement, it might be argued that the groups that operate as al-Qaeda affiliates, wannabes, and copycats have profited from the Arab uprisings in terms of expanding their operations and digging in, although in the process many have jettisoned many of the central tenets of the original cohort. This might be evolution, but it is just as likely to mark the deterioration or even the dissolution of the al-Qaeda wing of the jihadi movement. St. Matthew asked, "And what do you benefit if you gain the whole world but lose your own soul?" In the case of a number of al-Qaeda affiliates, wannabes, and copycats, you become just another gang.

And an extremely unpopular one at that. According to the Pew Research Global Attitudes Project,[6] public support for al-Qaeda (that is, al-Qaeda central and its affiliates that have kept the faith) throughout the Muslim world reached an all-time low in 2013: 57 percent of those surveyed held an unfavorable view of the organization and only 13 percent a favorable one. Support for suicide bombings followed the same trend. To top it off, 67 percent expressed concern about Islamist extremism in their countries. Al-Qaeda is clearly losing the battle for hearts and minds.

Will the state system in the Arab world survive the Arab uprisings?

Since the uprising in Syria evolved into a civil war which spilled over its boundaries into Lebanon and Iraq, and since the Islamic State established a caliphate that combines territory belonging to both Syria and Iraq, there has been a lot of talk about the artificiality of borders in the Middle East (as if all borders aren't artificial) and the "end of Sykes-Picot" or "the end of the Sykes-Picot borders." The latter phrases refer to a secret agreement negotiated during World War I by two diplomats, Sir Mark Sykes, representing the British, and François Georges-Picot, representing the French (the Russians later signed on as well). The agreement divided the territory that is now central and southern Turkey, Israel, Palestine, Jordan,

Iraq, and eastern Arabia into zones of direct and indirect British and French control, along with an international zone around Jerusalem and a Russian zone in Turkey.

Although those who have used the term run the gamut from Osama bin Laden to various journalists, it is a misnomer. Today's borders bear only the slightest relationship to those drawn up by the two diplomats. The French and Russians did not end up with chunks of territory carved out of present-day Turkey, the British did not get direct control over the eastern Arabian Peninsula, Jerusalem was never internationalized, and the mostly horizontal divisions demarcating various zones of control appear more like a crazy quilt of paint swatches when drawn on a map than anything a geographer would recognize today. The actual borders in the eastern Arab world came after the war and not during it. This is just one more example of why historical metaphors should be left to historians.

But all this begs the question: Are we witnessing the end of the state system in the Arab world that, with the exception of two Yemens consolidating into one in 1990, has been with us for forty years or so?

Two factors contributed to the durability of that state system. First, the passage of time. Although most member states of the state system in the region received their complete independence after World War II, the process of formulating distinct national identities began even while those states were under colonial or mandatory rule (two obvious outliers being Yemen and Libya). Ever since, states engaged their citizens in common practices and worked to develop their own internal markets and divisions of labor—necessary preconditions for the formation of distinct national identities. The states in the region also jealously guarded their borders, rewrote their histories, and, indeed, produced enough of their own histories to differentiate their national experience from that of their neighbors. The second factor that maintained the state system was big power intervention, which protected states from their enemies, both foreign and domestic. Whenever some strongman rose to the surface threatening to upset the regional balance of power, he was slapped down by one or another great power or coalition. This is exactly what happened to Saddam Hussein in 1991 when he attempted to integrate Kuwait into Iraq.

Events that unfolded after the outbreak of the Arab uprisings in 2010–11 have complicated this picture somewhat. When it comes to strengthening or diminishing national identities in the various states of the Arab world, the effects of the uprisings and protests have been dissimilar. As demonstrated by the popularity of patriotic rap and hip-hop music, the uprisings reaffirmed distinct Tunisian and Egyptian national identities. On the other hand, it is entirely possible that Yemen and, perhaps, Libya will fragment, with each fragment ordering itself in a manner appropriate for joining the world system of nation-states, much as South Sudan did when it broke away from Sudan in 2011. Then there are the cases of Syria and Iraq, where sectarian and ethnic identities are likely to trump national identity.

Sectarian movements resemble nationalist movements but differ on one critical point: As opposed to nationalists, sectarians do not seek sovereignty, only autonomy or rights within the national community. Thus, a sectarianized Syria and Iraq offers no challenge to the Arab state system as it now stands. And it is unlikely that the international community will allow the fragmentation of Syria or Iraq simply because it considers failed states better than shattered ones, particularly when their fragmentation is likely to have regional implications (a testament to the marginal importance of Yemen and Libya to the regional order). Hence, the international community bears up with the fiction that is Somalia.

The caliphate announced by the Islamic State is intentionally designed to throw a monkey wrench into the Arab state system. What better way to foil the designs of the Crusader-Zionist conspiracy than ignoring its handiwork? Nevertheless, the survival of this or any other "anti-state" that might arise in the future is unlikely. Such entities are incapable of mobilizing the human and material resources that have allowed modern states to endure and elbow out most other forms of political community. The populations they seek to rule are habituated to the role modern states play in their daily lives. And as the international coalition brought together against the Islamic State demonstrates, great powers and their regional allies which could not tolerate the attempts made by Gamal Abd al-Nasser or Saddam Hussein to change the map of the region by charisma or force are unlikely to give ground to the disruptive presence of the Islamic State's caliphate in a region as important as the heartland of the eastern Arab world.

How did the spread of the uprisings to Palestine affect the Israeli–Palestinian conflict?

The "Kerry round" of face-to-face negotiations between Israelis and Palestinians collapsed in April 2014 and therefore changed little in terms of the dynamics of the conflict. However, the overlooked uprising in the Palestinian territories may open up a new chapter in the history of the struggle.

For over forty years, the target of Palestinian acts of resistance was Israel, a foreign power that had occupied the Palestinian territories in 1967. While much of the world focused on the violence commonly perpetrated by small cells of fedayeen (literally, "self-sacrificers") and Islamist militants, beginning with the first intifada in 1987 Palestinians pioneered many of the techniques of protest that their Arab brethren would take advantage of during the 2010–11 uprisings: "people power"-style mobilizations, nonviolent civil disobedience, land reoccupations, and the like. With the onset of the uprisings, nonviolent protests continued as well. For example, in 2012 the Israeli government announced it was formulating plans to build housing in an area bordering on

East Jerusalem—claimed by the Palestinians as the site of their future capital. In response, Palestinian protesters set up a tent city "Bab al-Shams" ("Gate to the Sun") to block construction. By March 2013 polls revealed that close to 60 percent of Palestinians supported a nonviolent popular uprising against Israel.

Around the time of the uprisings, however, Palestinians not only challenged the Israeli occupation but their own leadership as well. A group calling itself "Gaza Youth Breaks Out" posted a Facebook manifesto calling for a reconciliation between the two main Palestinian factions—the Palestine Liberation Organization, which dominated the governing Palestinian Authority (PA) in the West Bank, and Hamas, which governed Gaza—that were at loggerheads, and another group called for a Day of Rage on March 15 to the same end. Thousands participated.

The most serious protests against the PA broke out in the West Bank in September 2012 after the prime minister, Salam Fayyad, raised prices on food and fuel. Although Fayyad rivals within the PA helped mobilize crowds, the protests took on a life of their own, becoming in the process truly popular. Spurred on by the same sort of labor activism that had proved decisive in the Egyptian uprising, Palestinians quickly escalated their demands from the economic to the political, calling for the firing of Fayyad (and, in some cases, the resignation of the president of the PA, Mahmoud Abbas), the abolition of the PA, the end of negotiations with Israel, and the establishment of a Palestinian state within the 1967 borders with East Jerusalem as its capital. The protests deeply shook the leadership of the PA.

Forced to respond, Mahmoud Abbas decided to seize the initiative by taking the Palestinian case for statehood to the United Nations. Abbas had attempted to achieve recognition for a Palestinian state in the UN Security Council the year before—a fool's errand, since the United States, which saw this as an end run around the negotiations it was so anxious to broker, could, if pressed, use its veto power to block it there. This time, however, the West Bank leadership decided to take its case to the UN General Assembly. Although Palestine could at best achieve the status of a "non-voting member entity" through the General Assembly—a form of quasi-recognition also granted the Vatican—the members of the assembly were overwhelmingly supportive of the Palestinian cause.

In the end, 138 members of the General Assembly voted for changing Palestine's status, forty-one abstained, and only seven joined Israel and the United States in voting no. In January 2013, the Palestinian Authority officially declared itself the State of Palestine and Mahmoud Abbas became its first president.

Having the same status as the Vatican in the United Nations might seem like a poor consolation prize, but it does come with some benefits: it allows the Palestinians, should they choose, to avail themselves of some of the advantages open to independent states. Included among them is membership in international organizations, including the International Court of Justice. Should the Palestinians be admitted to the court, they would have the option of putting Israel on the docket, since the West Bank upon which Israel has been expanding now constitutes part of a sovereign state and is not, as Israeli jurists would have it, "disputed." Recognition also gives legal sanction for other states to take individual action against Israel, such as imposing sanctions or participating in boycotts.

Just as important, however, the Palestinian bid for UN recognition is meaningful as much for what it signifies as it is for what it might accomplish. After years of fruitless negotiations with Israel, the Palestinians now had the option of walking away from the bargaining table and going it alone.

What can history tell us about "revolutionary waves"?

Ever since the Egyptian uprising, when events in one country (Tunisia) found a receptive audience in another (Egypt), historians and other social scientists have looked to the past to explore other "revolutionary waves" that might help explain current events and instruct us about the course those events might take. In chronological order, the most common historical analogies are: 1789, the kick-off date for the French Revolution, which spread notions of "liberty, equality, fraternity" among subjugated populations throughout Europe; 1848, the "Springtime of Nations"; 1968, when a wave of "youth revolutions" demanding an end to social and political hierarchies (to oversimplify a bit) engulfed France, Mexico, the United States, and Japan, among others; and 1989, when the Berlin Wall fell and Soviet domination of central and eastern Europe ended.

For his part, President Obama has been studying the close to sixty "people power" uprisings of the 1980s, such as the ones which occurred in the Philippines, South Korea, and Indonesia. And while we are at it, what about the wave of constitutional revolutions that broke out around the turn of the twentieth century, when rebels in the Ottoman Empire, Persia, Egypt, Russia, Mexico, Japan, and China demanded a written contract with their rulers specifying their rights?

The list of possible analogies seems endless, depending on what particular characteristics and outcomes one wishes to highlight and what particular characteristics and outcomes one wishes to forget. It is doubtful, for example, that Obama is looking for lessons from the first of the so-called people power revolutions—the 1978–79 Islamic revolution in Iran—or from the Palestinian *intifada*, which broke out in 1987. Instead, he has chosen his revolutions on the basis of their demands (an end to authoritarian rule and a more open system) rather than their tactics (which is, after all, what people power is all about).

Then there is the problem of thinking of historical parallels while riding the revolutionary roller coaster. During the winter of 2011, when the uprisings in the Arab world were spreading seemingly without limit and the focus was on those social-networking youths, the most popular analogy was 1989.

Over time, as the reality of the staying power of regimes, popular backlash against the failures of newly installed governments, and the problems that lie ahead sank in, 1848 seems to have overtaken 1989 as a reference point among historians. None of the revolutions that broke out that year overthrew monarchs and established more open, liberal systems of governance, nor did they win independence for the "newly awakened" nations of Europe—two of their main goals.

Then again, the revolutions of 1848 might be read in an altogether different way. Although none of the revolutions in that bleak year succeeded, their outbreak signaled in retrospect that the field of political struggle in Europe had opened up to include liberal and nationalist alternatives to the old order. If we substitute "human and democratic rights" for "liberal and nationalist alternatives," we might say the same about the uprisings in the Arab world, thus replacing the gloomy narrative that is all too common today with one that is more heartening and realistic.

Have the uprisings spread beyond the Arab world?

In the spring of 2013, protesters occupied Gezi Park in the heart of Istanbul to protest government plans to demolish the park and build in its stead a shopping mall. Protests in Turkey spread, as did the issues at stake. Of particular concern to many protesters was what they perceived to be the growing authoritarianism and high-handedness of Prime Minister Recep Tayyip Erdogan and fears of growing Islamization of institutions and laws at the hands of the ruling Islamist party.

Turkey was not alone in experiencing an "occupy movement." About two years earlier, Spanish protesters had occupied Puerta del Sol, a square in central Madrid, in response to the government's austerity policies, unemployment, and their exclusion from the political process, among other issues. A few months later, it was Israel's turn. Protesters, complaining about the high cost of housing and the deterioration of social services, took over parts of Rothschild Boulevard in Tel Aviv. And in November 2011, Occupy Wall Street protesters set up encampments, first in Zuccotti Park in Manhattan, then in various other American cities. At issue was the role played by corporate America, particularly the financial industry, in politics, corporate greed, and a level of income inequality that put the United States on par with Mexico.

Protesters throughout the world claimed to have been inspired by the occupation of Tahrir Square during the Egyptian uprising (another indication of the power of the myth). Setting aside the problem with wave theories discussed in Chapter 1—that they shift responsibility away from those who choose to do something and place it on some mysterious force that compels them to act—could it be that the Arab uprisings had transcended the boundaries of the Arab world and had become global in scope?

There are a number of similarities the various occupy movements share with the Tahrir Square occupation (or at least the myth) and with each other. There is the age profile of the protesters, their use of social media to mobilize and inform, their democratic structure, their tactic of laying claim to public space as a demonstration of empowerment, and their refusal to accept the status quo. Furthermore, all the protests targeted, directly or indirectly, the neoliberalization of the protesters' lives, from the privatization of public space and austerity measures imposed by a government to the way the free market has driven up housing costs and the widening disparity in wealth between "the 1 percent" and "the 99 percent."

On the other hand, there are significant differences as well among the occupy movements, including their grievances and demands, the targets of their anger, the social status of participants, the use of violent/nonviolent tactics, and their staying power. There are also significant differences between the occupy movements and the Tahrir Square protests. Most important, not one of the occupy protests demanded the overthrow of the regime and all of them took place in states with democratically elected governments (yes, Turkey too). In the Turkish and American cases, they failed to mobilize, or even register with, a vast majority of the population. Their demands were often amorphous or scattered, as were their targets. And they could be surprisingly nonpolitical: the Rothschild Boulevard protesters refused to take a stand on what is perhaps the most important issue in Israeli politics— settlements and the disposition of the occupied territories— for fear of splitting the movement.

As in the case of historical analogies, whether one views the occupy movements as Tahrir Square gone global or as discrete events depends solely upon the characteristics and outcomes on which one chooses to focus.

When will we be able to judge the significance of the Arab uprisings?

As anyone who has studied European history can tell you, the French Revolution began in 1789 with the storming of the Bastille and ended in 1799 with the coronation of Napoleon as emperor. At least, that is the most common narrative. Other narratives are, of course, possible. What about beginning the story of the French Revolution in the early eighteenth century, with the spread of Enlightenment ideas, or during the reign of the centralizing Bourbon monarchs? After all, "liberty, equality, fraternity" was a product of the Enlightenment, and arguably the greatest accomplishment of the French Revolution was the centralization of France, which the Bourbons did so much to further. And what about ending the story of the French Revolution in 1945, when French women voted for the first time, thus fulfilling the revolution's promise of equality and political rights for all?

If one focuses on battles and treaties, the American Revolution lasted from 1776 to 1783, which is the way the story is commonly told. On the other hand, the eminent scholar of American history Gordon S. Wood focused on the radical social transformation the American Revolution brought about. His American Revolution began in 1760 or so and ended in the early nineteenth century.[7]

Historians invent narratives to tell a story. Like all stories, they must have a beginning, a climax, and an end. And like many stories, they tend to have a moral. Choose your moral and you get your beginning, climax, and end.

What conclusions might we draw from the uprisings so far?

Assuming we adopt the common narrative of the French Revolution and date it from the storming of the Bastille to the coronation of Napoleon as emperor, we are dealing with events that unfolded over the course of an entire decade. Only a fraction of that time has passed since the Tunisian street vendor Muhammad Bouazizi set himself on fire, and, as of this writing, events in the Arab world are still unfolding at a remarkable speed. Although it is still too early to gain the distance from events that historians need to render judgments, here is my top ten list of what we have learned from the uprisings so far:

1. Uprisings are extraordinary events, and being extraordinary they defy prediction.
2. Although the "imagined community" Arabs share with one another is remarkably robust, the site of political action in the Arab world remains the nation-state.
3. The path taken by an uprising depends upon four factors: state institutions and capabilities, the ability of the opposition to maintain a broad and unified coalition, the cohesiveness of the military and the side it takes, and the intervention (or lack of intervention) of outside powers.
4. The longevity of a post-uprising government—whether the opposition or the old regime wins the initial

scrimmaging—depends upon its willingness and ability to reach out to those on the other side.

5. The Arab world has not been impervious to norms of human and democratic rights that have spread globally since the 1970s, nor has culture or religion prevented aspirations for those rights in the region.

6. The role played by social media in the uprisings was overblown.

7. On the other hand, the role which economics has played and will continue to play in shaping the outcome of the uprisings has been underappreciated.

8. Since neoliberal policies sparked widespread anger throughout the region, further neoliberal policies are unlikely to defuse it.

9. The spontaneity, leaderlessness, diversity, and loose organization that have marked the uprisings have been both their greatest strength and their greatest liability.

10. Whatever the rhetoric, the default position of American foreign policy remains expediency.

NOTES

Chapter 1

1. The full text of the reports can be found at http://hdr.undp.org/ xmlsearch/reportSearch?y=*&c=r:Arab+States&t=*&lang=en&k =&orderby=year (accessed June 6, 2014).

2. http://graphics.eiu.com/PDF/Democracy_Index_2010_web.pdf.

3. http://www.defense.gov/news/newsarticle.aspx?id=44863.

4. http://www.imf.org/external/np/g8/052611.htm. The phrase "Middle East and North Africa" is not equivalent to the phrase "Arab world" because it includes non-Arab majority states such as Turkey, Israel, and Iran. Although the report does not define what is meant by the phrase, it appears to be concerned with the Arab world.

5. Clement M. Henry, *The Mediterranean Debt Crescent: Money and Power in Algeria, Egypt, Morocco, Tunisia, and Turkey* (Gainesville: University of Florida Press, 1996).

6. http://www.cato.org/event.php?eventid=3729.

7. The United Nations has chosen the ages fifteen to twenty-nine to define *youth* because most countries divide their data into five-year increments.

8. http://www.shababinclusion.org/content/document/ detail/559/.

9. http://www.businessinsider.com/governments-food-price-inflation-2011-1.

10. Daniel Patrick Moynihan, "The United States in Opposition," *Commentary* (March 1, 1975), http://www.commentarymagazine.com/article/the-united-states-in-opposition/.

11. Samuel P. Huntington, *The Third Wave: Democratization in the Late Twentieth Century* (Norman: University of Oklahoma Press, 1993).

12. Hussein Ibish, "Was the Arab Spring Worth It?," *Foreign Policy* (June 9, 2014); F. Gregory Gause, III, "The Year the Arab Spring Went Bad," *Foreign Policy* (December 31, 2012), http://www.foreignpolicy.com/articles/2012/12/31/the_year_the_arab_spring_went_bad?page=full; Marc Lynch, "How Syria Ruined the Arab Spring," *Foreign Policy* (May 3, 2013), http://www.foreignpolicy.com/articles/2013/05/03/how_syria_ruined_the_arab_spring.

Chapter 2

1. Cited in Kenneth J. Perkins, *A History of Modern Tunisia* (Cambridge, UK: Cambridge University Press, 2004), 197.

2. http://www.economist.com/node/12202321?Story_ID=E1_TNNDNPNT.

3. See John Sfakianakis, "The Whales of the Nile: Networks, Businessmen, and Bureaucrats during the Era of Privatization in Egypt," in *Networks of Privilege in the Middle East: The Politics of Economic Reform Revisited*, ed. Steven Heydemann (New York: Palgrave Macmillan, 2004), 77–100.

4. http://middleeast.about.com/od/tunisia/a/tunisia-corruption-wikileaks.htm.

5. http://www.foreignaffairs.com/articles/67348/carrie-rosefsky-wickham/the-muslim-brotherhood-after-mubarak.

6. David Hearst, "Muslim Brotherhood Urged to Share Power in Egypt," *The Guardian*, June 12, 2014, http://www.theguardian.com/world/2012/jun/12/muslim-brotherhood-share-power-egypt.

7. Cited in Benjamin Barthe, "Meet the Three Young Men who Decided to Oust Mohammed Morsi," *Worldcrunch*, July 21, 2013,

http://www.worldcrunch.com/default/meet-the-three-y oung-men-who-decided-to-oust-mohammed-morsi/ revolution-tamarod-tahir-muslim-brotherhood/c0s12829/#. U1LFlFftCZ4.

Chapter 3

1. http://alsalamest.com/Ahmar_profile.pdf.
2. http://www.telegraph.co.uk/news/wikileaks-files/libya-wikileaks/8294920/AL-QADHAFI-THE-PHILOSOPHER-K ING-KEEPS-HIS-HAND-IN.html.
3. http://nymag.com/news/politics/saif-qaddafi-2011-5/index4. html.
4. http://www.crisisgroup.org/~/media/Files/Middle%20 East%20North%20Africa/North%20Africa/107%20-%20 Popular%20Protest%20in%20North%20Africa%20and %20the%20Middle%20East%20V%20-%20Making%20Sense%20 of%20Libya.pdf; http://www.jadaliyya.com/pages/index/1001/ is-the-2011-libyan-revolution-an-exception; http://www.lebanon-wire.com/1103MLN/110341612MER.asp.

Chapter 4

1. http://www.transparency.org/cpi2010/in_detail.
2. To the best of my knowledge, the term *coup-proofing* was invented by RAND Corporation analyst James T. Quinlivan in 1999. See his "Coup-Proofing: Its Practice and Consequences in the Middle East," *International Security* 24 (Autumn 1999): 131–65.
3. https://www.cia.gov/library/publications/world-leaders-1/ BA.html
4. http://www.hrw.org/en/news/2010/10/20/bahrain-elections-t ake-place-amid-crackdown.
5. http://articles.cnn.com/2011-05-31/world/syria.tortured. child_1_security-forces-damascus-body?_s=PM:WORLD.
6. http://www.foreignpolicy.com/articles/2013/11/21/rebels_inc.

7. https://www.middleeastmonitor.com/articles/middle-east/10055-the-evacuation-of-homs-humanitarianism-or-ethnic-cleansing.

Chapter 5

1. http://www.jadaliyya.com/pages/index/818/demands-of-saudi-youth-for-the-future-of-the-nation.

2. http://www.newyorker.com/reporting/2011/05/02/110502fa_fact_lizza.

3. http://www.whitehouse.gov/the-press-office/remarks-president-acceptance-nobel-peace-prize.

4. http://www.ned.org/george-w-bush/remarks-by-president-george-w-bush-at-the-20th-anniversary.

5. See Abu Bakr Naji, *The Management of Savagery: The Most Critical Stage Through Which the Umma Will Pass*, trans. William McCants (Cambridge, MA: John M. Olin Institute for Strategic Studies, 2006), 28.

6. http://www.pewglobal.org/2013/09/10/muslim-publics-share-concerns-about-extremist-groups/.

7. Gordon S. Wood, *The Radicalism of the American Revolution* (New York: Vintage, 1993).

FURTHER READING

General Works on the Middle East

Beinin, Joel. *Workers and Peasants in the Modern Middle East.* Cambridge, UK: Cambridge University Press, 2001.

Gelvin, James L. *The Modern Middle East: A History,* 4th ed. New York: Oxford University Press, 2015.

Henry, Clement M., and Robert Springborg. *Globalization and the Politics of Development in the Middle East.* Cambridge, UK: Cambridge University Press, 2001.

Insider Accounts

Alhassen, Maytha, and Ahmed Shihab-Eldin, eds. *Demanding Dignity: Young Voices from the Front Lines of the Arab Revolutions.* Ashland, OR: White Cloud Press, 2012.

Ghonim, Wael. *Revolution 2.0: The Power of the People is Greater than the People in Power: A Memoir.* Boston: Houghton Mifflin Harcourt, 2012.

Weddady, Nasser, and Sohrab Ahmari, eds. *Arab Spring Dreams: The Next Generation Speaks out for Freedom and Justice from North Africa to Iran.* Basingstoke, UK: Palgrave Macmillan, 2012.

Yazbek, Samar. *A Woman in the Crossfire: Diaries of the Syrian Revolution.* London: Haus Publishing, 2012.

al-Zubaidi, Layla, and Matthew Cassel, eds. *Diaries of an Unfinished Revolution: Voices from Tunis to Damascus.* New York: Penguin Books, 2013.

Edited Volumes

Council on Foreign Relations, ed. *The New Arab Revolt: What it Means and What Comes Next.* New York: Council on Foreign Relations, 2011.

Gerges, Fawaz, ed. *The New Middle East: Protest and Revolution in the Arab World.* New York: Cambridge University Press, 2013.

Haddad, Bassam, et al. *The Dawn of the Arab Uprisings: End of an Old Order?* London: Pluto Press, 2012.

Lesch, David W., and Mark L. Haas, eds. *The Arab Spring: Change and Resistance in the Middle East.* Boulder, CO: Westview Press, 2012.

Other

Alexander, Christopher. *Tunisia: Stability and Reform in the Modern Maghreb.* Milton Park, Abingdon, UK: Routledge, 2010.

Boucek, Christopher, and Marina Ottaway. *Yemen on the Brink.* Washington, DC: Carnegie Endowment for International Peace, 2010.

Brownlee, Jason. *Democracy Prevention: The Politics of the U.S.–Egyptian Alliance.* New York: Cambridge University Press, 2012.

Hashemi, Nader, and Danny Postel. *The Syria Dilemma.* Boston: Boston Review Books, 2013.

El-Kikhia, Mansour O. *Libya's Qaddafi: The Politics of Contradiction.* Gainesville: University Press of Florida, 1997.

Matthiesen, Toby. *Sectarian Gulf: Bahrain, Saudi Arabia, and the Arab Spring that Wasn't.* Stanford, CA: Stanford University Press, 2013.

Osman, Tarek. *Egypt on the Brink: From Nasser to Mubarak.* New Haven, CT: Yale University Press, 2010.

Owen, Roger. *The Rise and Fall of Arab Presidents for Life.* Cambridge, MA: Harvard University Press, 2012.

Wickham, Carrie Rosefsky. *The Muslim Brotherhood: Evolution of an Islamist Movement.* Princeton: Princeton University Press, 2013.

WEBSITES

Foreign Policy

www.foreignpolicy.com

International affairs periodical with contributions from top experts.

International Crisis Group

www.crisisgroup.org

Independent analysis of conflicts and potential conflicts in Middle East and beyond.

Jadaliyya

www.jadaliyya.com

Ezine of the Arab Studies Institute, covering culture, politics, and economics of the Arab world.

al-Jazeera (English)

http://english.aljazeera.net

English language site of the widely read Arabic language newspaper.

Middle East Research and Information Project (MERIP)

http://www.merip.org

Online edition of alternative news source on the Middle East.

INDEX

Abaza, Amin, 46
Abbas, Mahmoud, 179–180
Abdullah (king of Jordan), 158–160
Abu Salim prison riots (Libya),
    91–92, 100
Adel, Muhammad, 59
Aden (Yemen), 94, 99
Adwa (Egypt), 82
Afghanistan, 143, 146, 154, 166
agriculture, 22–23
Ahmar family (Yemen), 88–89,
    99, 107
Alawite sect, 2, 40, 119, 121, 130–131,
    144–145, 147–148
Aleppo (Syria), 127, 131
Alevi population (Turkey), 151
Alexandria (Egypt), 51–53
Alexandria Charter (2004), 33
Algeria, 1, 5, 13, 30, 33, 68
    Berbers in, 2, 34
    Black October riots (1988) in, 34
    debt burden in, 16
    food and food crises in, 21, 23
    human rights abuses in, 6, 30
    IMF riots (1988) in, 18
    presidential terms in, 5
    state of emergency in, 6
allocation states, 8
American aid. *See also* United
    States
    to Egypt, 8, 14, 69
    as source of rent, 8

American Revolution, 184–185
Amnesty International, 146
annual per capita income in Arab
    world, 10–11
Ansar al-Sharia (Libya), 108, 111,
    114, 174
Ansar al-Sharia (Tunisia), 67, 174
anticolonial populism, 13–14
April 6 Youth Movement (Egypt),
    27–28, 51–54, 56, 58–59, 63, 66,
    82, 183
Arab Charter on Human Rights
    (1994), 32
Arab Fund for Social and Economic
    Development, 3
*Arab Human Development Report
    2002*, 4–5
*Arab Human Development Report
    2004*, 16
Arabic language media, 3. *See also*
    al-Jazeera
Arab-Israeli War (1967), 118, 165,
    169, 178
Arab-Israeli War (1973), 68
Arab League, 3, 7, 32–33, 105,
    151–152
Arab monarchies. *See also specific
    countries*
    British role in the creation of, 12,
    155–156
    demands of protesters in, 158
    endurance of, 155, 157

Arab monarchies (*Cont.*)
  Gulf Cooperation Council and,
    100, 160
  number of, 155
  political party bans in, 6
  protests in, 158
Arab Monetary Fund, 3
Arab nationalism, 3
Arab socialism, 6, 14–16
Arab Spring, 37–38, 170. *See also*
    Arab uprisings
Arab uprisings, 55–56, 59–64, 77–79,
    81, 171, 177, 181. *See also under*
    specific countries
  Arab economies on eve of,
    10–12, 19, 23
  brittleness of regimes and, 25, 28
  demands for democracy and, 27,
    127, 132, 158, 166, 173, 182
  demands for human rights and,
    27–28, 32–33, 122, 166, 173, 182
  finding causes for, 25–28, 49–50,
    85
  Gulf Cooperation Council
    and, 100
  Israel-Palestine conflict and,
    178–180
  nonviolent resistance and, 50,
    57–59, 173
  political life on the eve of, 4–7,
    25, 34–35
  preliminary conclusions
    regarding, 172, 184–186
  al-Qaeda and, 172–175
  U.S. policy toward, 11, 166–170
  violence in, 84, 99, 101–103, 114
  wave metaphor to describe, 35–36
  youth bulge and, 21
Arab world, 27, 33, 39, 68, 98, 118,
    165, 175–178. *See also specific*
    countries
  Arab identity and, 2–4, 185
  Arab language and, 1–2
  authoritarianism in, 7–10
  censorship in, 6
  Christians in, 2, 40, 119, 130,
    147–148
  defined, 1

  economic conditions on
    the eve of uprisings in,
    10–12, 19, 23
  economic development
    policies in, 13
  labor activism in, 19
  linguistic and ethnic
    minorities in, 2
  monarchies in, 155–164
  Muslim sects in, 1–2
  national dialogues in, 47
  neoliberal policies in, 17–18, 86
  opposition to U.S. policies in, 3,
    58, 67, 108
  political life on eve of uprisings
    in, 4–7, 25, 34–35
  regional associations in, 3
  regional development funds and,
    3
  rentier states in, 8–9
  ruling bargains in, 13, 15–18,
    25, 28
  state of emergency laws in, 6, 63,
    71, 76, 82, 126, 129
  state security courts in, 6
  wave metaphor to describe
    protests in, 35–36
  youth population in, 19–21
Assad, Bashar al-, 120–122, 128,
    134, 141, 150–152, 158, 160,
    168–169, 174
Assad, Hafez al-, 34, 118, 120, 128,
    144, 158, 169
Assad, Maher al-, 121
authoritarianism, 7–10. *See also*
    under specific states

Baath Party (Syria), 3, 128–129
Baghdad (Iraq), Islamic State attack
    (2014) on, 138
Baghdadi, Abu Bakr al-,
    138–139, 174
Bahrain, 1, 34, 40, 118, 141, 163, 173
  American Fifth Fleet in, 117
  Day of Rage protests (2011) in, 122
  Great Britain and, 117
  guest workers in, 116
  human rights abuses in, 6, 122

monarchy in, 28, 116, 120,
124–125, 155
national dialogue in, 47, 124–125
oil and oil revenues in, 116
outside intervention in, 124, 160,
168–169
political naturalization in,
121–122
protests in, 26, 123, 125
Shi'i majority in, 2, 119, 121–122,
124–126
uprising (2011) in, 26, 28, 119,
122–126, 159, 170, 173
Baida (Syria), 130–131
baltagiya, 44, 71, 98, 122–123
Banias (Syria), 127, 130–131
Ban Ki-moon, 142
Banna, Hassan al-, 64
bedouin, 52
Ben Ali, Zine al-Abidine, 43, 79
corruption under, 45, 72
departure from power of, 26–27,
47–48, 63, 68, 72, 96, 98
as Tunisia's president, 27, 42–45,
47–48, 60
Ben Bella, Ahmed, 30
benefits for compliance, 9
Benghazi (Libya), 100, 103–104, 108,
111, 114
Berbers, 2, 34, 111, 158
Berber Spring (Algeria, 1980), 34
Berlusconi, Silvio, 102
bin Laden, Osama, 112, 114, 172–174
biofuels, 23
"black-hole states," 5
Black October riots (Algeria, 1988),
34
"Blue Revolution" (Kuwait,
2002–2005), 35
Bonaparte, Napoleon, 184–185
Bosnia, 105
Bouazizi, Muhammad, 27, 46–47,
49–50, 185
Bourguiba, Habib, 42–43, 60, 68
Brahimi, Lakhdar, 152
Brazil, 23
bread riots, 23
Britain. See Great Britain

"bunga-bunga parties," 102
Bush, George W.
freedom agenda of, 10, 37, 167,
170–172
Middle East foreign policy
of, 166

Cairo (Egypt). See Tahrir Square
(Cairo)
Cairo University, 15
Canada, 24
Carter, Jimmy, 31
Cedar Revolution (Lebanon, 2005),
35, 37, 170
Center for Applied Non-Violent
Action and Strategies
(CANVAS), 59
Central Security Services
(Egypt), 44
Charter 77, 32
Chechnya, 154
Chile, 80
China, 12, 23, 55, 91, 115, 181
Churchill, Winston, 156
Civil Forum, 32
climate change, 23
Clinton, Hillary, 141
cold war, 9–10, 29, 31, 118
Comoros, 1, 159
constitutional revolutions, 181
Coptic Christians, 2, 40
corn, 23–24
corruption, 5, 7, 116, 127, 134,
139,158
neoliberalism and, 18, 45–46
in Tunisia and Egypt, 18–19,
44–46, 55, 70, 72
in Yemen and Libya, 87–89, 92,
94, 109
"coup-proofing," 119–122
crony capitalism, 18, 45, 88–89. See
also corruption
"Crusader-Zionist conspiracy",
112–113, 136–137, 172–173, 177
Cuba, 31
cyberphiles and cyberskeptics,
55–57
Czechoslovakia, 32, 37

Damascus (Syria), 28, 83, 126–127, 131, 145
Damascus Declaration Movement (2005), 34
Damascus Spring (2000), 34, 128
Daraa (Syria), 127, 129–130
Darfur region (Sudan), 6
Day of Rage protests
    in Bahrain, 122
    in Egypt, 36
    in Gaza, 179
    in Libya, 28, 100
debt crisis (1980s), 16–17
debt relief, 17, 144
decolonization, 12–13, 29
De Gaulle, Charles, 104
"Demands of the Saudi Youth for the Future of the Nation" (manifesto), 158
democracy, 4, 7–8, 33, 35–36, 171, 186
    Damascus Declaration's call for, 34
    direct *versus* representative forms (Libya) and, 90
    "integral" form of, 15
    in Iraq, 7
    Islamist movements and, 67, 73
    "reactionary" forms of, 15
    as reason for Arab uprisings, 27, 127, 132, 158, 166, 173, 182
    Sadat's understanding of, 43
Djibouti, 1
Doha Declaration for Democracy and Reform (2004), 33
dollar inflation, 24
Duma (Syria), 127

The Economist, 7, 40
Egypt, 1, 13, 36–37, 89, 93–94, 118, 149, 164, 166, 181
    Arab socialism in, 14–16
    authoritarian rule in, 9–10, 41–42, 77–78
    constitution in, 5, 29, 43, 74, 76–78, 80
    Coptic Christians in, 2, 40
    corruption in, 18–19, 44–46, 70
    debt burden of, 16
    dependence on rent in, 8
    earlier protests in, 57–58
    economic development policies in, 14–15, 18
    economic growth in, 16
    economic inequality in, 40–41
    economic reform in, 18, 40
    food and food crises in, 21–23, 40
    Free Officers' coup (1952) in, 41–42, 68
    human rights abuses in, 6, 10, 71–72, 84–85
    IMF riots (1976) in, 18
    labor activism in, 19, 28, 51–54, 56, 58–59, 61–62, 71, 84, 179
    military's role in post-uprising government in, 67, 71, 75–81, 83
    military's role in uprising in, 42, 51, 53–54, 62, 67–71, 84–85, 96, 103
    monarchy in, 12, 43
    myths about uprising in, 84–85
    national dialogue in, 47
    neoliberal economic policies in, 40–41, 45, 61, 69–70, 81
    nonviolent character of uprising in, 50, 57, 173
    Obama and economic assistance to, 11
    political parties in, 5, 43, 53, 64, 66–67, 73, 78
    presidential terms in, 5
    Public Employment Guarantee Scheme in, 14–15
    "reactionary" *versus* "integral" democracy in, 15
    security forces in, 44, 53, 71–72
    state of emergency in, 6, 63, 71, 76, 82
    subsidies in, 15, 18, 23
    Supreme Council of the Armed Forces (SCAF) in, 28, 54, 62, 68, 71, 76
    Tunisia compared to, 39–46, 50–51, 68–75, 116
    unemployment in, 12, 14, 20

uprising (2011) in, 2–3, 9, 26, 28,
    39–40, 42, 45–46, 50–57, 59,
    61–63, 66–71, 78–79, 82–85, 96,
    98–99, 103, 108, 111, 120, 123,
    126, 157, 159–161, 167–168, 171,
    173, 177, 180, 183
  U.S. aid to, 8, 14, 69
  wheat imports and, 22
  youth population in, 20–21
Egypt Human Development Report
    2010, 56
Egypt Spinning and Weaving Plant
    (Mahalla al-Kubra, Egypt), 52,
    56, 58–59
Ennahda (Islamist party in Tunisia),
    62–63, 66–67, 72–75, 79
Equity and Reconciliation
    Commission (Morocco), 35
Erdogan, Recep Tayyip, 182
Essebsi, Béji Caïd, 72, 74
Euro-Mediterranean Free Trade
    Area, 18
European Union, 23, 104, 151. *See
    also specific countries*
  Libya and, 104
  Syria and, 160
Ezz, Ahmad, 46

Facebook. *See also* social media
  in Tunisia and Egypt, 47,
    51, 54–56
  "We are all Khaled Said"
    (Facebook page), 51, 54
Facebook Revolution, 54–55
Fayyad, Salam, 179
food
  food crises and uprisings,
    21–25, 28
  grain imports and, 23
  meat consumption and, 23–24
  prices for, 23–24
  security, 23–24
  subsides for, 15, 23, 179
  Syria's food supply, 22–23,
    142, 147
France
  Algeria's independence from,
    13, 68

elections in, 24, 104
Libya intervention (2011) and,
    103–104
Mali intervention (2013) and,
    113–114, 140
Morocco and, 156
role in creating Arab state system
    of, 12, 118, 156
Tunisia and, 41–42, 68, 104, 156
"youth revolution" protests (1968)
    in, 181
freedom agenda (Bush
    Administration), 10, 37, 167,
    170–172
Freedom and Justice Party (FJP,
    Egypt), 64, 73
Free Syrian Army (FSA), 134–135,
    141, 143
French Revolution, 25, 29, 49, 181,
    184–185
"Friends of Syria Group"
    (international coalition), 133,
    141–143

G -8, 11
Gafsa Phosphate Company protests
    (Tunisia), 60–61
Garrana, Zuhair, 46
Gaza, 6, 57–58, 162, 179
General National Council (GNC,
    Libya), 102, 111
Geneva Communiqué (Syrian civil
    war, 2012), 151–152
Geneva II talks (Syria conflict), 115,
    151–152, 169
Gezi Park protests (Turkey, 2013),
    182
Ghannouchi, Rachid, 73–74, 164
Ghonim, Wael, 54
Global Financial Crisis (2008), 24
"global war on terrorism," 10, 113,
    167–168
Great Britain, 24, 94, 157, 161,
    175–176
  creation of Jordan and, 12, 156
  East of Suez policy of, 117
  Egypt's conditional
    independence from, 41

Great Britain (*Cont.*)
   role in creating Gulf monarchies
      of, 12, 118, 155–156
Great Depression (1930s), 26
Greece, 24
Green Book (Qaddafi), 90–91, 102
Green Revolution (Iran, 2009),
      55–56, 144
gross domestic product (GDP)
      levels in Arab world, 11–12, 149
guest workers, 10, 95–96, 116, 161
Gulf Cooperation Council (GCC), 3,
      100, 124, 160
Gulf monarchies. *See* Arab
      monarchies
Gulf War (1991), 10, 22, 157

Hadi, Abdu Rabbu Mansour, 100,
      107, 110
Hamas, 162, 179
Hashemite Kingdom of Jordan.
      See Jordan
Hashid tribal confederation
      (Yemen), 88
Haykal, Muhammad, 79
Helsinki Accords (1975), 31–32
Heni, Chams Eddine, 49–50
Hizbullah, 117, 143–146, 148, 150, 163
Homs (Syria), 130–131, 145, 147
Houthi rebels (Yemen), 110
humanitarian intervention, 105–106
human rights, 34–35, 171. *See also*
      under specific countries
   Arab uprisings' demand for,
      27–28, 32–33, 122, 166, 173, 182
   disappeared prisoners and, 28,
      84–85, 92, 146
   as international norm, 26,
      29–30, 186
   Islam and, 7
   al-Qaeda and, 172
   United States and, 30–31,
      170, 172
Human Rights Watch, 32, 62, 122
Huntington, Samuel, 35–36
Hussein (sharif of Mecca), 156
Hussein, Saddam, 37, 120, 165,
      177–178

Iceland, 24
India, 94, 117, 156
Indonesia, 7–8, 21, 181
"integral democracy," 15
International Criminal Court, 29
International Crisis Group, 103
International Monetary
      Fund (IMF), 11, 14–15,
      17–18, 23
internet. *See* social media
intifada, 34, 57, 178, 181
Iran
   Bahrain and, 123–125, 163
   claim to regional leadership of,
      162–163
   Green Revolution (2009) in,
      55–56, 144
   Hizbullah's relations with,
      117, 163
   Islamic Revolution (1978–79) in,
      55–56, 165, 181
   Saudi Arabia and, 162–163
   Shi'ism in, 143–144
   Syria's alliance with, 117, 143–145,
      153–154, 162–163, 169
   United States' relations with, 154,
      162, 164–165
Iran-Iraq War (1980–1988), 144
Iraq, 1, 7, 13–14, 154, 157, 163
   "coup-proofing" under Saddam
      Hussein in, 120
   human rights abuses in, 6
   Islamic State (IS) and, 138–140,
      148, 151, 169–170, 173, 175
   Kurds in, 2, 140, 148
   Kuwait invaded (1990) by, 10,
      165, 177
   monarchy in, 12
   protests in, 151
   Shi'i population in, 2, 137, 140,
      150–151
   state of emergency in, 6
   Sunni population in, 137, 139–140,
      150–151
   Syria and, 148–151, 169, 175
   tribes in, 140, 151
   U.S. withdrawal of troops from,
      166

U.S. invasion and occupation
   (2003–2012) of, 3, 37, 58, 136–137,
   140, 171
Ireland, 24
Islah Party (Yemen), 89, 107
Islamic Front (Syria), 133–136, 143
Islamic Pan-African Brigade
   (Libya), 101
Islamic State (IS)
   caliphate proclaimed by, 138–139,
      172, 174, 177
   divisions within, 139
   in Iraq, 138–140, 148, 151, 169–170,
      173, 175
   Jabhat al-Nusra and, 135, 138–139
   al-Qaeda and, 137–139, 174
   enforcement of Islamic law by,
      139, 174
   in Syria, 138–141, 143, 148, 151,
      153, 169, 173–175
   takfiri doctrine of, 136
   United States response to,
      169–170, 178
Islamists, 5, 27, 33–35, 57, 62–65, 70,
      73–84, 91, 107–108, 111, 129–130,
      133–136, 138–140, 143, 150, 182,
Israel, 67–69, 89, 145, 165–166,
      175, 179, 182–183. *See also*
      Israel-Palestine conflict
   occupation of the West Bank
      and Gaza Strip by, 57–58, 178,
      180, 184
   Syria and, 117–118, 129, 144,
      148, 169
   United States support for, 3, 9, 31
Israel-Palestine conflict, 57, 181
   Arab uprisings and, 178–180
   U.S. policy and, 3, 164–167,
      179–180
Istanbul (Turkey), 182
Italy, 94, 102
   elections in, 24
   Libya colonized by, 94
   Libya's oil imports to, 104

Jabhat al-Nusra
   Islamic State (IS) and, 135,
      138–139

al-Qaeda and, 135–136,
      138–139, 174
   Syrian civil war and, 143, 153, 174
   United States and, 143
jamahiriya ("rule by the masses,"
      Libya), 90, 95
Japan, 181
Jawlani, Muhammad al-, 138
al-Jazeera, 3, 47–49, 160
Jerusalem, 176, 178–179
jihad, 67, 136–137, 173–174
jihadi salafism, 67
Joint Meeting Parties (JMP, Yemen),
      97–99, 107
Jordan (Hashemite Kingdom of), 1,
      4, 118, 148–149, 175
   British occupation (1958) of, 157
   debt burden in, 16
   economic development
      policies of, 14
   economic concessions to
      protesters in, 159
   food crises in, 23
   Gulf Cooperation Council and,
      160
   human rights abuses in, 6
   IMF riots (1988 and 1996) in, 18
   Islamist political parties in, 33
   monarchy in, 12, 28, 155–156,
      158–160
   political parties in, 5
   protests in, 158–160
   unemployment in, 12
   youth population in, 21

Karman, Tawakol, 107
Kasserine (Tunisia), 48
Kefaya ("enough") coalition
      (Egypt), 35, 58, 65, 77
Kerry, John, 168, 178
Khalifa family (Bahrain), 117–118,
      120–121
Khatib, Hamza al-, 129–130
Kurds, 2, 35, 140–141, 148, 151–152
Kuwait, 1, 4, 35, 155, 161
   human rights abuses in, 6
   Iraq's invasion (1990) of, 10,
      165, 177

Kuwait (*Cont.*)
  monarchy in, 155
  oil revenues in, 161
  parliament in, 159
  Shi'is in, 2
  women's suffrage in, 35, 37

labor activism, 49, 94, 109
  in Egypt, 19, 28, 51–54, 56, 58–59,
    61–62, 71, 84, 179
  neoliberalism and, 61
  in Tunisia, 19, 49, 51, 59–61, 84
Latakia (Syria), 127
League of Nations, 118, 156
Lebanon, 1, 6–7, 117, 144–145,
    154, 159
  Cedar Revolution (2005) in, 35,
    37, 170
  elections postponed (2013) in, 150
  food crises in, 21–23
  French mandate and legacy in,
    12, 118
  IMF riots (1987) in, 18
  Maronite Christians in, 2
  Shi'is in, 2, 150
  Syria and, 35, 148–150, 165,
    169, 175
  unemployment in, 12
Lend-Lease program, 10
Lenin, Vladimir, 82
Libya, 1, 10, 13–14, 65, 86, 160
  Ansar al-Sharia in, 108, 111,
    114, 174
  Berbers in, 2, 111
  Day of Rage protest (2011) in,
    28, 100
  divisions and future stability in,
    42, 106–109, 111–112, 177
  economic development
    policies in, 18
  emigration from, 104
  food crises in, 21
  "Free Officers" coup (1969) in, 89
  General National Council (GNC,
    Libya), 102, 111
  human rights abuses in, 28–29,
    91–92, 102
  Italian colonization of, 94

  monarchy in, 94
  national identity in, 93–94,
    176–177
  NATO intervention (2011) in, 101,
    104–107, 115, 145, 168, 170
  neoliberalism in, 18
  oil and oil revenues in, 91, 94–95,
    104, 109, 159
  political life before the uprising
    in, 89–92
  political party ban in, 6, 90
  political repression in, 91–92
  post-uprising governments and
    politics in, 106–109, 111–112, 114
  rebels in, 101, 107–108, 115
  tribal system in, 92, 96–97,
    101–103, 111
  United Nations Security Council
    and, 105–106, 115
  United States and, 103–105,
    114–115, 143, 168, 170
  uprising (2011) in, 2, 96, 100–103,
    105–106, 109, 114–115, 120, 126,
    159, 170, 173
  violence of uprising in, 101,
    102–103, 114
  as a weak state, 92–97, 113
  youth population in, 20
Libyan National Army (LNA,
    militia), 111
Libyan Shield brigades, 111
Libyan Transitional National
    Council, 107
Lockerbie (Scotland), Pan Am
    bombing (1988) over, 102
Luxor Massacre (Egypt, 1997), 63

Madrid (Spain), 182
Mahalla al-Kubra (Egypt), 52,
    56, 58–59
Mahfouz, Asmaa, 51
Mali, 113–114, 140
Maliki, Nouri al-, 139–140, 150
Manama (Bahrain), 122–124
MANPADS (man-portable
    air-defense systems), 142–143
Mansour, Adli, 78
Mao Zedong, 91

Maronite Christians, 2
Mauritania, 1, 6
meat consumption, 23–24
"Mediterranean debt crescent," 17
Mesopotamia, 22
Mexico, 181, 183
middle class in the Arab world,
    19, 33, 39
Military Operations Command
    (Syria), 135
Milosevic, Slobodan, 59
Minya (Egypt), 82
Moldova, 55–56
Monastir (Tunisia), 48–49
Morocco
    Berbers in, 2, 158
    constitutional changes in, 158
    debt burden in, 16
    food crises in, 21–23
    Gulf Cooperation Council and,
        160
    human rights abuses in, 6, 35
    IMF riots (1983) in, 18
    monarchy in, 12, 28, 155–156, 158
    nationalist movement in, 156
    "Years of Lead" in, 35
Morsi, Muhammad
    Egyptian judiciary and, 76–77
    Egyptian military and, 76
    executive power expanded by,
        71, 76–77
    governance record of, 73–77, 80
    indictment of, 82
    al-Jazeera's coverage of, 160
    military coup deposing (2013), 67,
        77–78, 80, 83, 85, 168
    military's suppression of
        supporters of, 81–82
    presidential election (2012)
        of, 64
    Saudi Arabia and, 161
    Sisi and, 76
    United States and, 161, 168
Moscow Helsinki Watch Group, 32
Mosul (Iraq), 138–140
Mubarak, Gamal, 45–46, 70, 89
Mubarak, Hosni, 43, 58, 61, 66, 83
    corruption under, 45–46

departure from power of, 26,
    28, 54, 62, 68, 70, 75, 84–85, 96,
    161, 168
Free Officers' Coup as origins of
    regime of, 42
indictment against, 71
response to Egyptian uprising
    of, 53–54
security apparatus under, 44, 53
United States and departure from
    power of, 161, 167–168
United States' collaboration with,
    10, 167–168, 171
Muhammad (prophet), 2, 66
Muslim Brotherhood (Egypt), 33,
    51–52, 63–67, 73–83, 111, 161,
    164, 168
Muslim Brotherhood (Syria), 129,
    133, 164
Myanmar, 62

Nasser, Gamal Abd al-, 165, 178
    economic policies of, 14–15
    as Egypt's president, 41–43, 69
    Muslim Brotherhood and, 64
    Qaddafi's imitation of, 89–90
National Coalition for Syrian
    Revolutionary and Opposition
    Forces, 133–134, 141, 143
National Coordination Committee
    for the Forces for Democratic
    Change (NCC, Syria), 133–134
National Democratic Party (NDP,
    Egypt), 53
National Dialogue Conference
    (Yemen), 100, 106
National Guard (Bahrain), 122
national identity in Arab world, 3,
    176–178
Neo-Destour Party (Tunisia), 60
neoliberalism, 17–18, 22–23, 30,
    40–41, 45–46, 61, 69–70, 81, 166,
    177, 183, 186
Netherlands, 24
Nicaragua, 31
Nida Tounis, 72–74
Nigeria, 146
nizam, definition of, 25

Nomura (bank), 21
nonviolent resistance, 50, 57–59, 103, 123, 173, 178–179
North Africa, 1, 11–12, 19, 113–114, 149, 172. *See also specific countries*
North Atlantic Treaty Organization (NATO) Libya intervention (2011), 101, 104–107, 115, 145, 168, 170
North Yemen (Yemen Arab Republic), 86–87, 110
al-Nour Party (Egypt), 66–67, 78

Obama, Barack, 161, 166, 181
  Arab uprisings and, 11, 167–168
  on economic assistance to Arab states, 11, 23
  Islamic State (IS) and, 169–170
  Israel-Palestine conflict and, 164, 166–167
  Libya intervention (2011) and, 104, 143, 168
  Syrian uprising and civil war (2011–) and, 134–135, 143, 162, 165, 168–169
Occupy movements, 183–184
oil, 11–12, 116, 135, 141, 158, 161, 163
  European imports from Libya and, 104
  Iranian sales to Syria of, 144
  Libya and, 91, 94–95, 104, 109, 159
  ownership of, 17
  price fluctuations for, 16–17, 29, 91, 165
  as source of rent, 8
  United States foreign policy and, 9, 31, 104, 157
  United States' imports of, 9, 104
  Yemen and, 95, 110
Oman, 1, 86, 155
"Orange Revolution" (Kuwait, 2006), 35
Orascom, 89
Organization of Petroleum Exporting Countries (OPEC), 165
Orthodox Christians, 2

Otpor, 59
Ottoman Empire, 41, 118, 181

Pakistan, 146, 172
Palestine Liberation Organization (PLO), 179
Palestinian Authority (PA), 179–180
Palestinians. *See also* Israel-Palestine conflict; Palestinian Territories
  Arab world support for, 3, 30, 57
  Israel's negotiations with, 178–180
Palestinian Territories, 1, 6–7, 32, 57–58, 118, 156, 162, 175, 178–181, 184. *See also* Gaza; West Bank
pan-African unity, 90
Pan Am flight 103 bombing (1988), 102
pan-Arabism, 3, 90, 165
patriarchy, 7
Pearl Square (Manama, Bahrain), 123–125
"Peninsula Shield" (Gulf Cooperation Council military force), 124
"People Power Revolution" (Philippines, 1986), 55
People's Democratic Republic of Yemen (South Yemen), 86, 94
Pew Research Global Attitudes Project, 175
Philippines, 55, 181
Picot, François Georges, 175
"Pink Revolution" (Yemen), 98
Poland, 31
"political naturalization" (Bahrain), 121–122
political parties. *See also specific political parties*
  in Arab world as a whole, 3, 5–6
  in Gulf states, 6
  pan-Arabism and, 3
"Political Reform in the Middle East and North Africa" (Obama memorandum), 167
population demographics

in Arab world as a whole, 19–20, 28
in Egypt, 20–21, 39
in Libya, 20
in Russia, 21
in Tunisia, 20, 39
youth bulges and, 19–20
Port Said (Egypt) soccer violence
(2012), 72
Portugal, 24
Prague Spring (1968), 37
privatization
corruption and, 18, 45–46
neoliberalism and, 17–18, 40, 45
in Syria, 19
in Tunisia and Egypt, 18–19,
40–41, 45–46, 61
in Yemen, 88–89

Qaboos (sultan of Oman), 86
Qaddafi, Hannibal, 102
Qaddafi, Muammar, 10, 86, 93,
95–97, 104, 109, 171
corruption under, 89, 94
death of, 101, 106
Green Book of, 90–91, 102
International Criminal Court
indictment against, 29
Libya uprising (2011) and, 101,
107, 115
megalomania of, 89–90
Nasser as role model for, 89–90
political repression under,
91–92, 111
sanity of, 101–102
Third Universal Theory of, 90
titles of, 90
Qaddafi, Saif al-Islam, 95, 102–103
al-Qaeda, 112–114, 129, 135–139, 143,
146, 154, 172–175, 177
al-Qaeda in the Arabian Peninsula
affiliate and, 112–113, 172
al-Qaeda in Iraq affiliate, 137–138
al-Qaeda in the Islamic Maghreb
affiliate and, 113, 172
al-Qaeda in Mesopotamia affiliate,
172
Qatar, 1, 3, 111, 133, 135, 142, 155, 157,
159–160, 162, 164

annual per capita income in, 10
guest workers in, 10, 161
monarchy in, 155
oil revenues in, 161, 163
origins of, 117
Qatif (Saudi Arabia), 159
al-Qusayr (Syria), 145

R2P. See Responsibility to Protect
Raqqa (Syria), 138–139
"reactionary democracy," 15
Reagan, Ronald, 17, 31, 102
remittances, 95–96
rent, 8–9
rentier states, 8
Responsibility to Protect (R2P),
105–106
Revolutionary Committees
Movement (Libya), 91
revolutionary waves, 35, 180–181
Riyadh (Saudi Arabia), 157–158
"Rojava" (Kurdish region in Syria),
140–141
Rothschild Boulevard protests (Tel
Aviv, Israel; 2011), 182–184
ruling bargains in the Arab world,
13, 15–18, 25, 28
Russia, 21, 80, 168
constitutional revolution in, 181
grain and, 23
Syria and, 115, 117, 133, 143, 145,
151–154, 162
United Nations Security Council
and, 115, 133, 145
youth population in, 21
Rwanda, 105

Sadat, Anwar al-, 43, 63, 69, 165–166
Said, Khaled, 51, 54
salafism, 65–67, 74, 112,
Saleh, Ali Abdullah
departure from power of, 26, 100,
106, 160
protests against, 98–99
salafism and, 112
as Yemen's president, 10, 86–89,
92–93, 95–100, 109–110, 171
Saleh, Ali Ahmed, 87

salmiyya (peaceful), 57
Samarra (Iraq), 137
Sana (Yemen), 97–99, 110
Sana Declaration (2004), 33
Sana University, 98
Sanusi, Abdullah al-, 91
Sarkozy, Nicolas, 104
Sa'ud, Abdulaziz ibn Abdul
  Rahman al-, 156
Saudi Arabia, 1, 7, 14, 111, 156
  Bahrain and, 116, 124, 160, 162,
    164, 168–169
  elections in, 37
  as food exporter, 22
  Gulf Cooperation Council and,
    100
  Gulf War (1991) and, 22
  human rights abuses in, 6
  Lend-Lease assistance to, 10
  monarchy in, 28, 155, 159
  neoliberal policies in, 18
  oil revenues in, 158–159, 161, 163
  protests in, 157–159
  al-Qaeda in the Arabian
    Peninsula and, 112
  Shi'is in, 2, 157–159
  Syria and, 129, 133, 135, 142, 153,
    160–162, 164
  United States and, 10, 161–162,
    164, 170
  Yemen and, 88, 160, 163, 168
self-immolations, 27, 46, 48–50
September 11, 2001 terrorist attacks,
  112, 114, 165
Serbia, 59
shabiha, 122, 130–131, 144
Shalish, Dhu al-Himma, 121
Shawkat, Assef, 121
Shi'is and Shi'ism, 1–2, 40, 94, 110,
  112, 119, 121–122, 124–126,
  130, 140, 145, 147–148, 150–151,
  157–159
Sidi Bouzid (Tunisia), 27, 47, 49
Sisi, Abd al-Fattah al-, 76, 78, 85
Slovakia, 24
social media, 36, 47–51, 54–58, 65,
  83–84, 98, 100, 122, 125–126,
  144, 157, 181, 183, 186

Somalia, 1, 105, 159, 177
South Korea, 181
South Sudan, 177
South Yemen (People's Democratic
  Republic of Yemen), 86, 94
Soviet Union, 9–10, 29, 31–32, 37, 118,
  143, 165, 181–182
Spain, 24, 182
Special Security Force Command
  (Bahrain), 122
"Springtime of Nations" (Europe,
  1848), 37, 181–182
"Statement of a Thousand" (Syria,
  2000), 34
state security courts in the Arab
  world, 6
sub-Saharan Africa, 12, 19, 104
Sudan
  Darfur region of, 6
  debt burden of, 16
  extrajudicial detentions in, 6
  food and food crises in, 21
  South Sudan's secession (2011)
    from, 177
  state of emergency in, 6
Suez (Egypt), 52–53, 117
Suez Canal, 8, 14
Suleiman, Omar, 54, 161
Sunnis and Sunnism, 1–2, 40,
  118–119, 121–122, 130–131, 137,
  139–140, 147–148, 150–151,
  163–164
Supreme Council of the Armed
  Forces (SCAF, Egypt), 28, 54, 62,
  68, 71, 76
Supreme Military Council (SMC,
  Syria), 134–135, 143
Surt (Libya), 101
Sykes-Picot Agreement, 175–176
Syria, 1, 5, 13–14, 19, 34, 62,
  116, 160
  Alawite sect in, 2, 40, 119, 121,
    130, 145
  Baath Party in, 3, 128–129
  chemical weapons and, 141, 143,
    145, 162, 165, 169
  Christians in, 119, 130, 147–148
  "coup-proofing" in, 119–121

death toll of uprising and civil
   war in, 146
debt burden an debt relief in,
   16, 144
dependence on rent in, 8
food crises in, 22–23, 142, 147
foreign intervention in, 133–134,
   141, 146, 162, 164
French mandate and legacy in,
   12, 118
Geneva Communiqué (2012) and,
   151–152
Geneva II talks and, 115,
   151–152, 169
human rights abuses in, 6, 26, 127,
   130, 132, 146
Iran's alliance with, 117, 143–145,
   153–154, 162–163, 169
Iraq and, 148–151, 169, 175
Islamic State (IS) and, 138–141,
   143, 148, 151, 153, 169, 173–175
Islamists and, 129–130, 133–136,
   138–140, 143, 150 117–118, 129,
   144, 148–149,169
Jabhat al-Nusra in, 135–136,
   138–139, 143, 153
Kurds in, 2
Lebanon and, 35, 148–150, 165,
   169, 175
military and security forces in,
   121–122, 127, 129–132, 144
militias in, 133–135, 141, 152
neoliberalism in, 18
obstacles to settlement in,
   151–154
opposition forces in, 132–136,
   142-143
refugees and, 142, 146–151
regional security and civil war
   in, 148–151
repression of protests in, 28, 127,
   129–132
sectarianism in, 147–149, 177
state of emergency in, 6, 126, 129
unemployment in, 12, 20–21, 119
United States and, 10, 114–115,
   118, 129, 134–135, 141–143, 145,
   151–153, 161–162, 165, 168–170

uprising and civil war (2011–)
   in, 2, 26, 28, 38, 83, 115, 119,
   126–135, 142, 146–149, 153, 159,
   162, 164–165, 168–170, 173–175
youth unemployment in, 20–21
Syrian Islamic Front, 133
Syrian Islamic Liberation Front, 133
Syrian National Coalition, 133–134,
   141, 143
Syrian National Council,
   133–134, 164
Syrian Observatory for Human
   Rights, 132, 146
Syrian Revolution 2011 against
   Bashar al-Assad (protest
   group), 126, 132
Syriatel, 19

Taghayr (Change) Square (Sana),
   98–99, 106
Tahrir Square (Cairo), 27–28, 36,
   51–54, 56, 58–59, 63, 66, 82–83,
   98, 123, 183–184
Tahrir Square (Sana), 98. *See
   also* Taghayr (Change)
   Square (Sana)
Taiz (Yemen), 98–99
takfiri, 136
The Taliban, 143
Tamarod (Rebellion) movement
   (Egypt), 77, 79
Tartus (Syria), 117, 154
al-Tawhid wal-Jihad (Iraq), 136–137
Tel Aviv (Israel), 182–184
Terbil, Fathi, 100, 107
Thala (Tunisia), 47–48
Thatcher, Margaret, 17
Third Universal Theory (Qaddafi),
   90
Third World, 29–30
thuwwar ("revolutionaries," Libya),
   101
Tobruk (Libya), 111
Trabelsi, Leila, 45–46, 72
tribes
   in Bahrain, 117
   definition of, 96
   in Iraq, 140, 151

tribes (*Cont.*)
  in Libya, 92, 96–97, 101–103, 111
  in Yemen, 88, 96–97, 99, 103,
    112–113
Trimech, Abdesslem, 48–50
Tripoli (Lebanon), 150
Tripoli (Libya), 91, 100–101, 108, 111
Trucial States, 155
Tunis, 67–68
Tunisia, 1, 5, 43, 65, 93–94, 116
  Ansar al-Sharia in, 67, 174
  authoritarian rule in, 41–42
  Berbers in, 2
  corruption in, 44–46, 55, 72
  Ennahda (Islamist party) and,
    62–63, 66–67, 72–75, 79
  food crises in, 21
  France and, 41–42, 68, 104, 156
  human rights abuses in, 6, 62–63
  IMF riots (1984) in, 18
  labor activism in, 19, 49, 51,
    59–61, 84
  military's role in uprising in, 42,
    51, 67–71, 96, 103
  national dialogue in, 47
  neoliberal policies in,
    40–41, 45–46
  Obama and economic
    assistance to, 11
  political parties in, 5, 62–63,
    66–67, 72–75, 79
  political repression in, 44, 62–63
  regime response to uprising in,
    47–48
  security apparatus in, 44, 48
  social media in, 47–50, 54–55,
    57, 157
  Sunni majority in, 40
  unemployment in, 12, 20, 47
  uprising (2010–2011) in, 9, 24,
    26–28, 39–40, 42, 45–52, 54–55,
    57, 59–62, 67–72, 83–84, 96, 98,
    103–104, 120, 157, 159–160, 164,
    167, 171, 173, 177, 180
  youth demographics in, 20
Tunisian Combat Group, 67
Tunisian League for Human
  Rights, 32

Tunis summit (Arab League, 2004),
  32–33
Turkey, 8, 80, 140, 175–176, 182, 184
  Syria and, 135, 148–151, 153
"Twitter Revolution," 54

Ukraine, 55, 154
Union Générale Tunisienne du
  Travail (UGTT), 60–62, 72–73
United Arab Emirates (UAE), 1, 111,
  157, 159–160, 163
  Bahrain and, 124, 160, 168–169
  Gulf Cooperation Council and,
    124
  monarchy in, 155
  oil revenues in, 161
  origins of, 117, 155
United Arab Republic, 118
United Kingdom. *See* Great Britain
United Nations. *See also* United
  Nations Security Council
  Chapter VII resolutions and, 145
  Development Programme, 4
  Geneva Comminqué (2012) and,
    151–152
  High Commission for Human
    Rights, 6
  Palestinian Territories and,
    179–180
United Nations Security Council
  Libya and, 105–106, 115
  Resolution 1973 and, 105, 115
  Responsibility to Protect (R2P)
    and, 105–106
United States, 22, 24, 26, 29, 31,
  100, 149, 154, 157, 164, 181,
  183–184
  aid to Egypt and, 8, 14, 69
  aid to region and, 8, 10–11,
    14, 23, 69
  anti-terrorism and, 10, 113
  Arab monarchies and
    authoritarian governments
    allied with, 9–10, 13
  Arab world opposition to policies
    of, 3, 58, 67, 108
  Bahrain and, 117, 124, 168–170
  biofuel production in, 23

Bush freedom agenda and, 10, 37,
    167, 170–172
democracy promotion and, 10,
    166, 170–172
influence in Arab world of, 164–166
Iraq invasion (2003) and
    occupation (2003–2012) by, 3, 37,
    58, 136–137, 140, 171
Islamic State (IS) and,
    169–170, 178
Israel-Palestine conflict and, 3,
    164–167, 179–180
Libya intervention (2011) and,
    103–105, 114–115, 143, 168, 170
neoliberalism and, 17, 30, 166
Responsibility to Protect (R2P)
    and, 105–106
Saudi Arabia and, 10, 161–162,
    164, 170
Syria and, 10, 114–115, 118, 129,
    134–135, 141–143, 145, 151–153,
    161–162, 165, 168–170
Universal Declaration of Human
    Rights (1948), 29

The Vatican, 180
Vietnam, 21

Wahhabism, 163
"waithood," 21
wave metaphor describing Arab
    uprisings, 35–36, 183
waves of democratization, 35–36
weak states, 92–97, 113
"We are all Khaled Said" (Facebook
    page), 51, 54
West Bank, 6, 57–58, 178, 179–180, 184
wheat, 22–24
Wickham, Carrie Rosefsky, 65
WikiLeaks, 45, 55, 92
women, 66–67, 76, 106–107, 136,
    139, 184
    in Kuwait, 35, 37
    marriage and, 20
    unemployment among, 20
    voting rights in the Arab world
        and, 34–35, 37
    in Yemen,

Wood, Gordon S., 184–185
World Bank, 13, 16–17, 23, 39–40
World Trade Organization
    (WTO), 18
World War I, 118, 156, 175–176
World War II, 10, 12, 94, 176

Yemen, 1, 6, 160, 163, 168, 170
    annual per capita income in,
        10–11
    constitution of, 5, 87, 89, 106–107
    corruption in, 87–89, 92, 109
    debt burden in, 16
    divisions and future stability in,
        106–110, 177
    food and food crises in, 23
    Gulf Cooperation Council and,
        100
    national dialogue in, 47, 98, 100,
        106–107
    national identity in, 93, 176–177
    political life before the uprising
        in, 86–89
    political parties in, 5, 89,
        97–99, 107
    al-Qaeda in the Arabian
        Peninsula and, 112–113, 172
    Republican Guard and Special
        Forces in, 87
    Shi'is in, 2, 94, 110, 112
    tribal system in, 88, 96–97, 99, 103,
        112–113
    unification of North and South
        Yemen and, 110, 176
    uprising (2011) in, 2, 26, 28,
        84, 87, 96–100, 103, 109,
        120, 173
    violence of uprising in, 99, 103
    as a weak state, 92–97, 113
Yemen Arab Republic (North
    Yemen), 86–87, 110
youth bulges, 19–20
youth population
    in Arab world, 19–21
    in Egypt, 20–21, 50–51, 84, 183
    in Libya, 20
    marriage crisis among, 21
    in Syria, 20–21, 83

youth population (*Cont.*)
  in Tunisia, 20, 50–51
  unemployment among, 20
youth revolutions (1968), 181

Zarqawi, Abu Musab al-,
  136–138
Zawahiri, Ayman al-, 138, 174
Zaydis, 94, 110, 112